ORGY PLUS MASSACRE

SEXY, SCARY & SENSATIONAL CINEMA

VOLUME I (1950-1956)

CREDITS

ORGY + MASSACRE V.1
ISBN 978-1-84068-696-8
Edited by G.H. Janus

https://black-gas.org
Published by Deicide Press 2024
In association with The Nocturne Group

Design by Broken Fang Cryptography
A Fabbrica Sodoma production

CONTENTS

FOREWORD	005
HORROR	007
MAYHEM	027
MYTH	055
SCI-FI	071
SEX	107
INDEX	133

THING
NICE

FOREWORD

After working with the Nocturne Group on two anthologies of material selected from their ongoing series of books on early cinema,[1] I was delighted when they offered me the chance to edit a new set of film books using photographs and previously unpublished texts from their post-1949 archive. This mass of material was originally to be developed for inclusion in their original series, but was set aside when it became clear that to produce books equally in-depth for the years 1950 onwards would take decades. Instead, I now have the opportunity to include a selection of these basic but still informative texts to enhance this collection of rare production stills.

As such, the ORGY PLUS MASSACRE series will present a visually-led sampling of sexy, scary and sensational cinema from the years 1950 to 1979, three of the most consequential decades in film history. It was during these years that global cinema came of age, not only in the technological sense but especially by way of pushing back the old restrictions of censorship, so much so that by the end of the 1960s, explicit sex and graphic violence had both become accepted in the mainstream. This new liberalism peaked in the mid-70s, when pretty much anything could be legally seen on commercially available film in one form in another, from picture houses to backstreet projection booths. Of course, this provoked an inevitable backlash in the 1980s, but ORGY PLUS MASSACRE will focus purely on these years when film-makers were free to express their most expansive, excessive and extreme visions on celluloid.

As the remit from my publisher was to keep these books affordable, I have edited Volume 1 to include just over 100 rare and unusual photographs, with accompanying texts, from the years 1950 to 1956. This period saw global cinema in full recovery from the recent world war, and the transition of pulp narratives towards a darker realm informed by fears born of the new atomic age and the horrors of the concentration camps. The book is divided into five sections: Horror, Mayhem (delinquency, crime, murder, atrocity), Myth (fantasies of the near and distant past), Science Fiction, and last but not least, Sex (nudity, sexploitation, pornography[2]). When a film falls into more than one category, as many do, the most dominant theme was chosen.

I now look forward to working on the next volumes of this series, with each one revealing how cinema grew sexier, scarier and more sensational with every passing year.

–G.H. Janus

1. The series from the Nocturne Group is entitled SHADOWS IN A PHANTOM EYE, and documents the years 1872 to 1949. I have edited two anthologies of material taken from the series, SATANIC SHADOWS and BEASTS AND BEAUTIES. These represent just a fraction of the content that the series, which runs to 15 volumes and well over 3,000 pages, has to offer.

2. Yes, even in 1950 loops of pornographic film were available, screened in the most clandestine venues or sold under counters, a situation which continued until Denmark led the legalization of such material from 1968 onwards.

SON OF DR. JEKYLL
Production: USA, 1951
Director: Seymour Friedman
Category: Horror

HORROR

MESA OF LOST WOMEN
Production: USA, 1951-3
Director: Herbert Tevos & Ron Ormond
Category: Horror/Science Fiction
Legendary "bad" movie about a mad doctor (Jackie Coogan) in the Mexican desert whose experiments with arachnids and humans seem to produce giant spiders, deadly long-nailed women, and male dwarfs. The film was originally directed by Tevos under the title **Tarantula** and completed in 1951; Ron Ormond acquired the unreleased footage and completely revamped it in 1952, under the working title **Lost Women Of Zarpa**. With dwarf star Angelo Rossito and several of his stunted friends leering and scampering around, plus the voluptuous Tandra Quinn dancing a wild tarantella, this film has all the freaked-out elements of an e-coli fever dream.

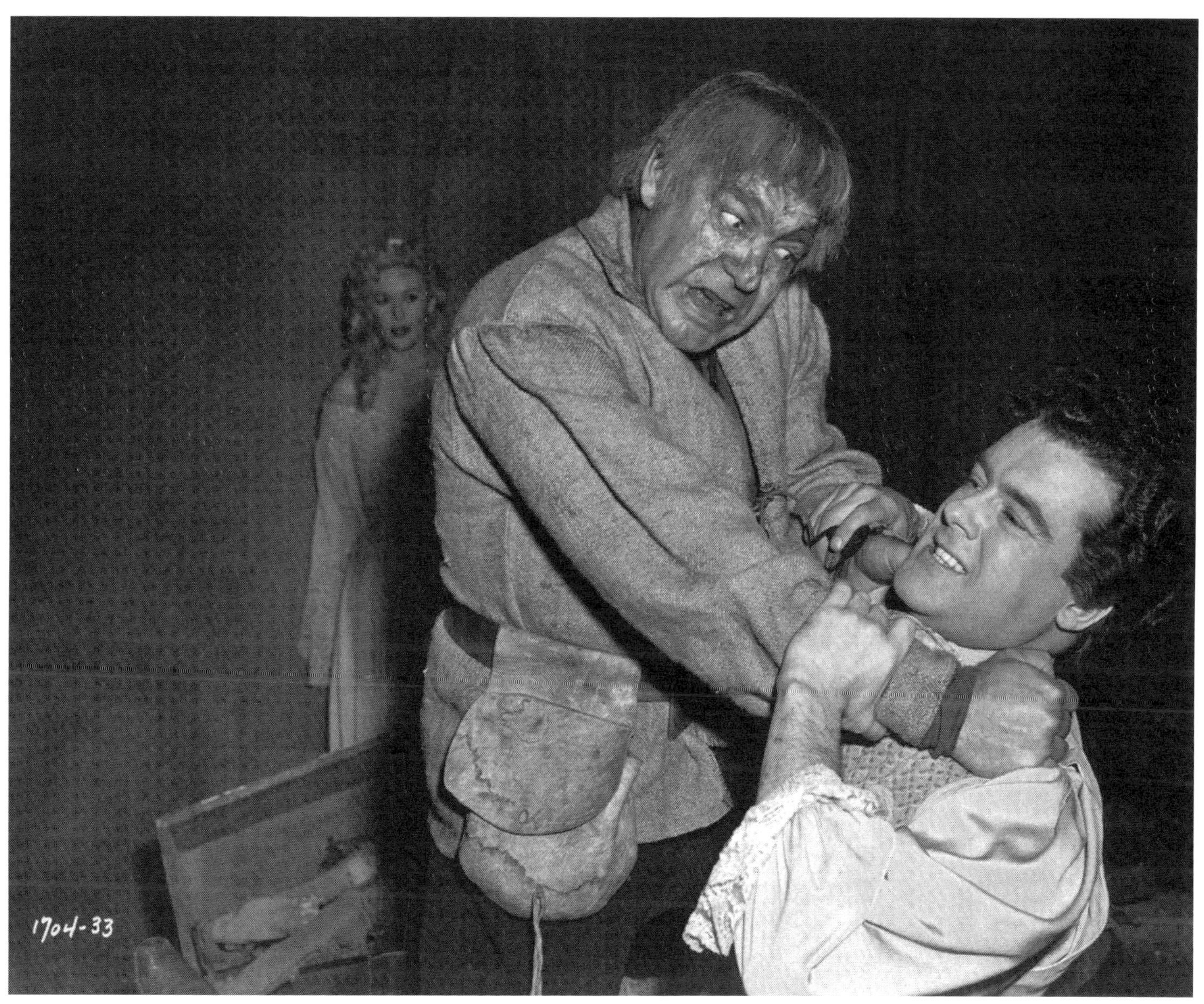

THE BLACK CASTLE
Production: USA, 1952
Director: Nathan Juran
Category: Historical Horror

NOITA PALAA ELÄMÄÄN
("The Witch Returns To Life")
Production: Finland, 1952
Director: Roland af Hällström
Category: Horror Fantasy

DEMENTIA
Production: USA, 1953
Director: John Parker
Category: Horror/Trance

A weird trance/horror experience, and one of the most effective uses of that archetypal signifier of the uncanny, the severed hand. Apparently Parker's only film, **Dementia** – denied release by censors until 1955 – uses shadow-bound techniques to show the strange, oneiric tale of a young madwoman. We see her wake up, meet a mysterious stranger, and through him get involved with an obese mobster (Z-movie doyen Bruno VeSota) who resembles her father – a violent man who she has already stabbed to death. She later kills the fat man in the same way, resorting to severing his dead hand when she realises it contains her pendant. We see her ditch the hand before the film leads us back to the first scene of the woman waking. We assume it has all been a dream, a simplistic explanation which is abruptly shattered when she opens her dresser drawer to reveal – the severed hand. A sinister dwarf newspaper vendor also appears (the ubiquitous Angelo Rossitto), explicitly referring us back to the distorted arena of Tod Browning's **Freaks**. A veritable catalogue of the uncanny filled with homicidal sexual abjection, human monsters, graveyard scenes and visions of phantom faces, **Dementia**'s drift is a Freudian shadow-key to the lock on a psychotic labyrinth. A recut 1957 version, by Jack Harris, was retitled **Daughter Of Horror**.

KAIBYO ARIMA GOTEN
("Ghost-Cat Of Arima Palace")
Production: Japan, 1953
Director: Ryohei Arai
Category: Horror/Cat-Ghosts

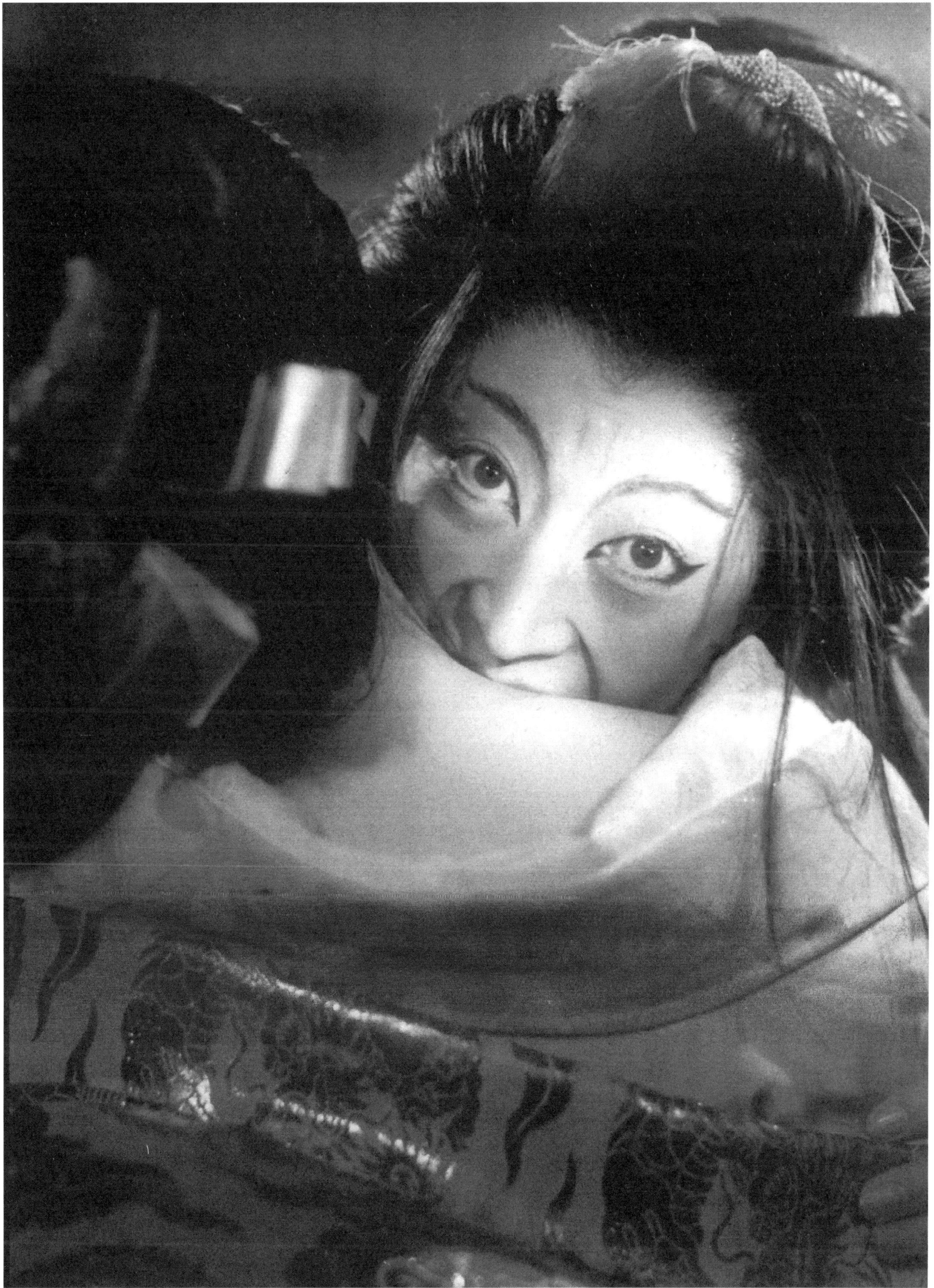

HOUSE OF WAX
Production: USA, 1953
Director: Andre de Toth
Category: Horror

A reworking of **Mystery Of The Wax Museum, House Of Wax** was an early 3-D feature directed by André de Toth and starring Vincent Price in his first major horror role. Although this version adds little new, Price is typically maniacal and boasts a great disfiguring make-up job by Gordon Bau; Charles Bronson plays Igor, his mute assistant. The film's climax, in which a naked young woman is threatened with being engulfed in molten wax, effectively taps into the bondage/torture fetish which was being more explicitly catered for by photographer Irving Klaw in the short underground sex films he was producing at that same time, items such as **Enslaved Brunette, Manacled Slave Maiden,** and **Leather Sheath Bondage.**

THE MAZE
Production: USA, 1953
Director: William Cameron Menzies
Category: Horror Fantasy
Menzies also designed the sets for this absurd, vaguely Lovecraftian gothic 3-D tale of a man who inherits a Scottish castle only to find that he must also look after one of his descendents, a biological freak who was born 200 years before as a man-sized frog. The film is somewhat redeemed by its outlandish scenography, the castle and maze coming to life in some darkly atmospheric moments. Menzies next designed and directed the SF classic **Invaders From Mars**.

EL MONSTRUO RESUCITADO
("The Resuscitated Monster")
Production: Mexico, 1953
Director: Chano Urueta
Category: Horror
Facial deformity and brain transplants are at the core of this tale in which a mad scientist resurrects a corpse to carry out his bidding. Urueta was one of Mexico's leading horror film directors.

THE BOWERY BOYS MEET THE MONSTERS
Production: USA, 1954
Director: Edward Bernds
Category: Horror/Comedy

GORILLA AT LARGE
Production: USA, 1954
Director: Harmon Jones
Category: Horror/Mystery

KAIBYO OKAZAKI SODO
("Ghost-Cat Mayhem At Okazaki")
Production: Japan, 1954
Director: Bin Kato
Category: Horror/Cat-Ghosts

THE MAD MAGICIAN
Production: USA, 1954
Director: John Brahm
Category: Horror
Starring Vincent Price and shot in 3-D, **The Mad Magician** was an obvious attempt to cash in on the success of **House Of Wax** from the previous year. Price plays a stage illusionist who uses his stage buzzsaw to perform real decapitations.

SATAN'S WAITIN'
Production: USA, 1954
Director: Friz Freleng
Category: Horror/Comedy
The most macabre and violent of the Freleng-directed Sylvester and Tweety cartoons, of which the first was **Tweetie Pie** (1947). At the start of the film, Sylvester is actually killed falling off a roof, and ends up in Hell where a satanic bulldog urges him to go out and lose his other eight lives. The next seven are duly forfeited in various ways – flattened by a steamroller, scared to death, and multiple shootings. With only one life left, Sylvester sees sense and flees to the presumed safety of a bank vault – only to be blown to bits by two incompetent robbers. The film ends with all three on the down escalator to damnation.

BRIDE OF THE MONSTER
Production: USA, 1955
Director: Edward D. Wood Jr.
Category: Horror/Science Fiction

CULT OF THE COBRA
Production: USA, 1955
Director: Francis D. Lyon
Category: Horror
Six GI's who witness the secret rites of a snake-woman cult in Asia are haunted by a fatal reptilian curse when they return home.

ISSUN-BOSHI
Production: Japan, 1955
Director: Seiichro Uchikawa
Category: Horror
One of several horrific films adapted from or inspired by the same-titled tale of grotesquerie by Edogawa Rampo. The deformed title creature is played by actor Tsutomo Wakui, also seen in the vampire horror **Onna Kyuketsuki** (1959). Issun-Boshi was originally the name of a tiny figure from Japanese myth.

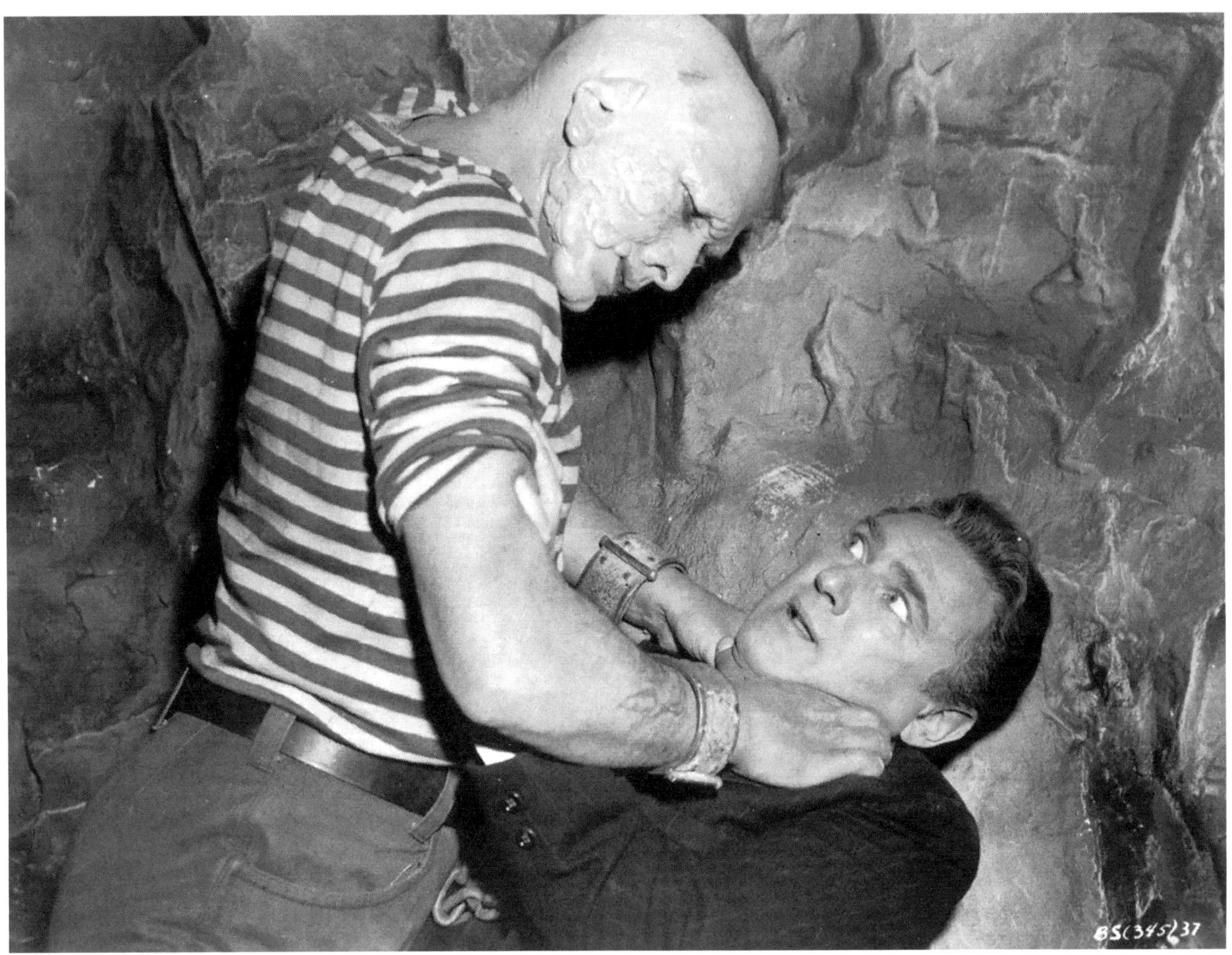

THE BLACK SLEEP
Production: USA, 1956
Director: Reginald LeBorg
Category: Horror
The cast includes Bela Lugosi (in one of his last movies), Basil Rathbone, Lon Chaney Jr (as Mongo, a retard), John Carradine and Ed Wood regular Tor Johnson. Rathbone is a doctor with a dungeon full of deformed mutants.

THE SHE-CREATURE
Production: USA, 1956
Director: Edward L. Cahn
Category: Horror

Bizarre, pelagic pulp nocturne of hypnotic regression, sexual obsession, and metempsychosis, in which a violent, female primeval creature is evoked from the ocean depths to do an evil svengali's murderous bidding. Another unsung classic from the phenomenal Cahn. The theme of hypnotic regression/reincarnation was also examined in other low-budget horror films of the period such as W. Lee Wilder's **Fright** (1956) and Roger Corman's awesome **The Undead** (1956).

THE UNDEAD
Production: USA, 1956
Director: Roger Corman
Category: Horror
Great horror movie with Satan, a witch, a dwarf (Billy Barty), beheadings, and a hooker under hypnosis.

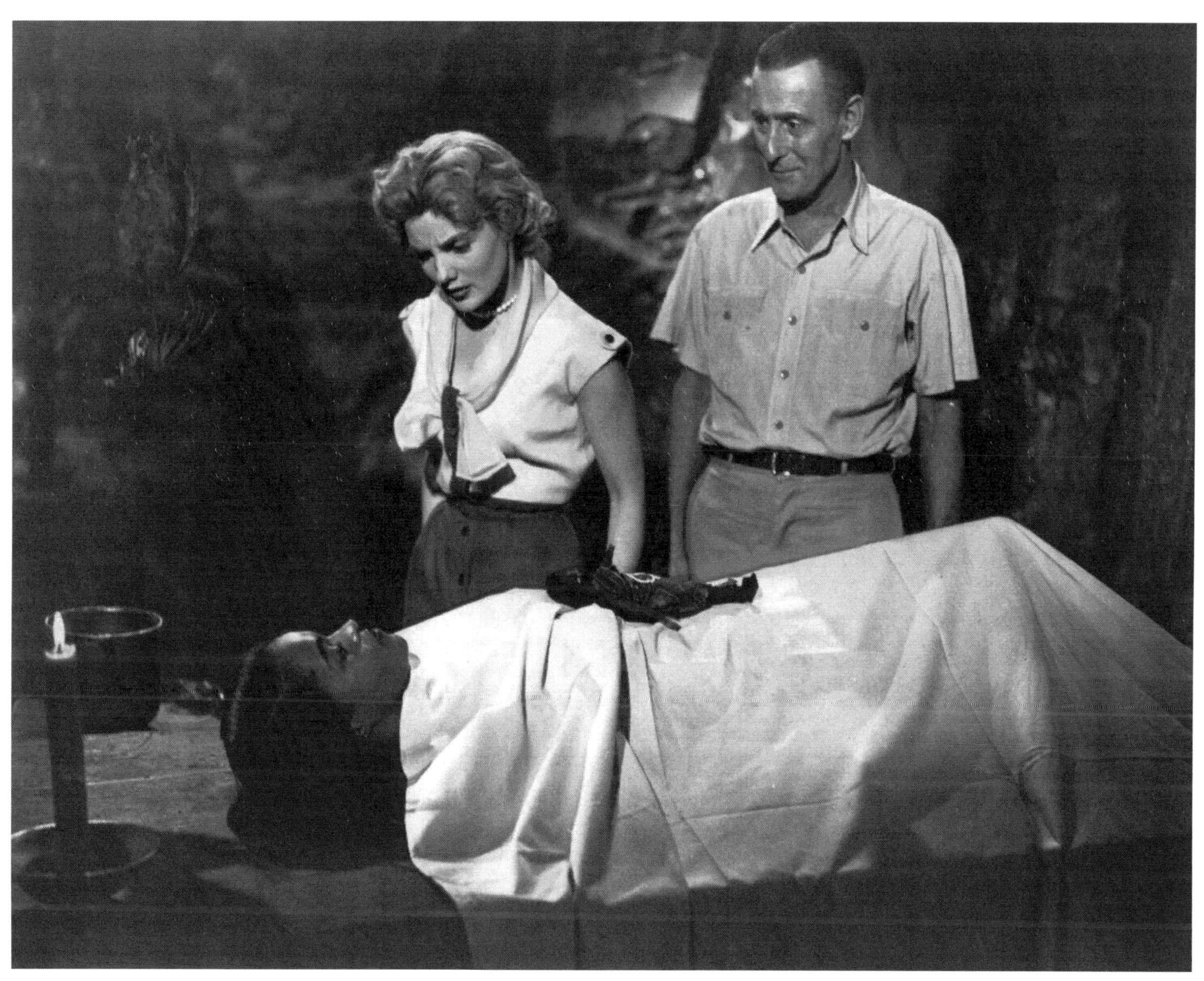

VOODOO WOMAN
Production: USA, 1956
Director: Edward L. Cahn
Category: Horror/Voodoo

CAGED
Production: USA, 1950
Director: John Cromwell
Category: Women In Prison

MAYHEM

MARIHUANA: EL TABACO NEGRO DEL DIABLO
("Marihuana: The Devil's Black Tobacco")
Production: Spain/Argentina, 1950
Director: León Klimovsky
Category: Drugs/Sleaze
An early piece of drug exploitation drama from Klimovsky, who would later become known for a series of lurid Spanish horror movies in the 1970s. Here, Pedro Lopez Lagar plays a surgeon out to avenge the murder of his wife, who was addicted to marihuana and died in sleazy circumstances. Entering the drugs underworld in search of justice, he fall prey to the evil weed himself and struggles to avoid a similar fate. With a trippy 3-D segment, this film was released in the USA as **Marihuana Story** and also known as **Slaves Of The Underworld.** It was remade, as **Humo De Marihuana**, in 1968.

LOS OLVIDADOS
("The Forgotten Ones")
Production: Mexico, 1950
Director: Luis Buñuel
Category: Crime
Relocating to Mexico after a period in Los Angeles, Buñuel set about creating a series of subversive feature films which employed standard narratives whilst enabling the Surrealist film-maker's penchant for cruel and unusual images. In **Los Olvidados**, Buñuel recreates the sadism of his early short films, featuring such scenes as a blind beggar surrounded by jeering youths, knocked over and robbed (typically, Buñuel confuses our sympathies by making the blind man a paedophile). In the same film, a legless man is lifted bodily from his cart, stumps waggling in the air, and hurled into the gutter. A reminder that much of Buñuel's lust for mayhem was derived from Sade came in the later **Él** (1953), whose protagonist, armed with rope, needles and thread, sets off to sew up his wife's sexual organs – a direct reference to the final act of Sade's *Philosophy In The Boudoir*, where Eugénie injects her mother's vulva with pox and then stitches it shut.

H – THE STORY OF A TEENAGE DRUG ADDICT
Production: USA, 1951
Director: Larry Frisch
Category: Drugs Admonitory
A 22-minute anti-drugs educational film, produced by Young America Films, in which a good kid named Bill is pressured into experimenting with drugs by a pusher, Roy, depicted as a stereotypical hep-cat hustler. Marijuana-smoking (at a hipster party) soon leads to heroin abuse and addiction; miraculously, Bill recovers at the end of the film. **H**, one of the very first anti-heroin films, is symptomatic of a growing concern at the start of the 50s that heroin addiction, once the sole province of poor, ghettoized blacks, was spreading to the young, white population through experimentation with other narcotic substances; this rising tide of dread was also helped along by the appearance of sensational exploitation novels, such as Hal Ellson's *The Golden Spike* (1952) and William [Burroughs] Lee's *Junk* (1953). Other 50s junkie movies include Bill Free's short **Teen-Age Menace** (1951), Charles Edwards and Irvin S. Yeaworth Jr.'s **The Flaming Teen-Age** (1956), and Alexander J. Wells'

Hooked (1958). **The Narcotics Story**, also from 1958, was actually a semi-documentary police training film which was appropriated and put into roadshow circulation.

THE TERRIBLE TRUTH

Production: USA, 1951
Director: Sid Davis
Category: Drugs Admonitory
One of Davis' first educational films, a 10-minute warning on the perils of drug experimentation. Teenager Phyllis dabbles in pot-smoking, and is soon talked into trying something harder, leading her into heroin addiction, theft, and drug-dealing; she is also raped, and lands herself a criminal record. In short, a few puffs of marijuana have effectively ruined her life. Davis also adds an element of "red scare", as the judge in the case proclaims that the Soviets are secretly sponsoring the illicit drug trade in America, in order to poison its youth. Other cautionary drugs films from the early 50s include **Subject Narcotics** (1951, with scenes of intravenous injection and references to prostitution), and **Narcosis**, a police film from 1954 depicting graphic drug withdrawal scenes.

GIRL GANG

Production: USA, 1952
Director: Robert C. Dertano
Category: Crime/Drugs
Produced by George Weiss (as Broadway Roadshow Productions) and directed by Dertano – a teaming which first emerged on the Z-grade crime/she-wrestling hybrid **Racket Girls** (1951, also known as **The Blonde Pick-Up** and **Pin Down Girls**), starring female grappler Peaches Page – **Girl Gang** may be the first commercial film which shows how to cook up and inject heroin in step-by-step stages. Gun violence also features, with multiple deaths. Weiss next dabbled in burlesque and nudism films, notably **Nudist Life** (1961) which was cobbled together from footage culled from 30s, 40s and 50s naturist features. **Girl Gang** was released in 1954, during the golden age of pulp fiction dealing with juvenile delinquency, teenage gangs, violence, drugs and sex, and appeared almost simultaneously with a classic of the genre, Wenzell Brown's *Gang Girl.*

THE HITCH HIKER
Production: USA, 1952
Director: Ida Lupino
Category: Serial Killer
A noirish psycho-killer movie, based on the true case of Billy Cook. Born in 1928, Cook was a cock-eyed runt, disowned by his parents, who ended up in reform school with a reptutation for extreme violence and anger. Released in 1950, he embarked on a murderous crime spree which involved mutiple car-jackings and kidnappings; moving from highay to highway, Cook left a trail of bullet-riddled corpses in his wake (including three children) until he was was finally arrested and executed in 1952. Shot by Nicholas Musuraca, **The Hitch-Hiker** utilises abandoned highways and bleak desertscapes to project a nihilistic aura of alienation as two travellers face summary death at the hands of the sadistic hitcher. Filmed in 1952, released 1953.

ONE-WAY TICKET TO HELL
Production: USA, 1952/56
Director: Bamlet L. Price Jr.
Category: Juvenile Delinquency/Drugs
Alternative Title: **Teenage Devil Dolls**

THE SNIPER
Production: USA, 1952
Director: Edward Dmytryk
Category: Serial Killer/True Crime
Eddy Miller (played by Arthur Franz) is quiet, polite young man who has a deadly secret: in his darkest moments, he takes a long-range rifle and shoots women dead from a safe distance. Director Dmytryk paints a picture of loneliness, sexual despair and growing madness utilising expressionistic camera angles and shadows, his warning of a slow-burning psychosis that one day erupts anticipating more renowned films of the 70s and 80s (such as **Taxi Driver**). The film was not a commercial success, perhaps because 50s audiences found its message hard to accept: that urban alienation and society's indifference to the mentally disturbed were the key causes of this killer's deadly actions. **The Sniper** was loosely modelled on the real-life case of Howard Unruh, an army-trained sniper who kept a diary detailing all his kills during WW2. Unruh carried his gun obsession back with him into civilian life, constructing a shooting-range in his basement and also, more disturbingly, keeping a list of people

he wished to "erase". He finally snapped on September 6, 1949, arming himself with two guns and running amok in his neighbourhood, killing thirteen people in as many minutes. He finally surrendered to police without a struggle, and was placed in a lunatic asylum for life.

THE BIG HEAT
Production: USA, 1953
Director: Fritz Lang
Category: Crime
Film noir, notorious for ramping up the genre levels of sadistic violence, particularly against women, and for its gloating focus on female facial disfigurement. In what becomes the film's key scene, Lee Marvin, enjoying his first significant role as a psychopathic hoodlum, hideously maims his girlfriend (Gloria Grahame) by hurling boiling coffee in her face. Lang's last American film of note; at the end of the decade he moved back to Germany to play out the end of his career.

LA SALAIRE DE LA PEUR
("The Wages Of Fear")
Production: France, 1953
Director: Henri-Georges Clouzot
Category: Suspense

IL VAMPIRO NEGRO
("The Black Vampire")
Production: Argentina, 1953
Director: Román Viñoly Barreto
Category: Serial Killer
Not blaxploitation, and not about vampires, this is a true crime film based on Fritz Haarmann, the blood-drinking butcher of Hannover.

MARLON BRANDO
D 8080-33

THE WILD ONE
Production: USA, 1953
Director: Laslo Benedek
Category: Bikers/Violence
In 1947, an event transpired in the small town of Hollister, California, which would lead to the media creation of a new type of delinquent – the motorcycle outlaw. When a group of bikers attending a rally got drunk and out of control, the story made the news and was, in many cases, blown out of all proportion. The perception of Hollister as a "riot" by "hoodlums" was cemented by the publication in 1951 of the story "Cyclists' Raid" by Frank Rooney; two years after that, the story became a film, **The Wild One**, starring Marlon Brando as Johnny, the archetypal black leather rebel biker, and a new sub-genre of exploitation film was born.

CELL 2455 DEATH ROW
Production: USA, 1954
Director: Fred F. Sears
Category: Crime/Prison
Based on the same-titled book by Caryl Chessman, the so-called "Red Light Bandit" who was sentenced to death for the robbery, rape and sodomizing of young women in 1940s Los Angeles. The death sentence was arrived at by a technicality, applying the "Little Lindbergh Law" that stated any crime that involved kidnapping with bodily harm could be considered a capital offense – the "kidnapping" in Chessman's case involved him dragging one girl a few yards from her car. Chessman proclaimed his innocence from day one, and stayed on Death Row for ten years, filing dozens of appeals and successfully avoiding eight execution deadlines; he also wrote four acclaimed books during that time. Despite pleas for clemency from literary figures including Aldous Huxley, Ray Bradbury, and Norman Mailer, Chessman was executed by gas chamber on May 2, 1960. His book *Cell 2455 Death Row* was also the basis for a Brazilian TV series, **Cela Da Morte** (1958), and Buzz Kulik's 1977 TV movie **Kill Me If You Can** was a dramatization of Chessman's case.

LES DIABOLIQUES
("The Fiends")
Production: France, 1954
Director: Henri-Georges Clozot
Category: Murder
Along with Hitchcock's **Psycho,** one of the most influential films ever made in terms of the cycle of 60s black-and-white shockers that included the likes of Hammer's **Paranoiac** and William Castle's **Strait-Jacket.**

THE FEMALE JUNGLE
Production: USA, 1954
Director: Bruno VeSota
Category: Murder-Noir

The first film directed by character actor VeSota also marked the screen debut of **Jayne Mansfield**, then working as a cinema usherette. Mansfield plays Candy Price, the mistress of a down-at-heel artist. Set entirely at night and plagued by monstrous shadows, VeSota's bizarre, low-budget film noir remains one of the strangest of the 1950s, fuelling rumours that he also directed parts, if not all, of the twisted masterpiece **Daughter Of Horror**, in which he also appeared that same year.

KD-(270)15

KISS ME DEADLY
Production: USA, 1954
Director: Robert Aldrich
Category: Atomic Noir
Ralph Meeker plays Mike Hammer, in the second film portrayal of pulp novelist Mickey Spillane's hard-hitting detective. Director Aldrich fuses elements of brutal crime, mystery, and even science fiction in this crowning film noir, which ends with an unexplained, but clearly apocalyptic, revelation. Hammer's first screen incarnation was in **I, The Jury** (1953), which opens with the savage 3-D slaughter of an amputee.

MAU MAU
Production: USA, 1954
Director: Elwood Price
Category: Documentary/Atrocity
This was a documentary, produced by Joe Rock and narrated by NBC newsman Chet Huntley, on the vicious Mau Mau uprisings against British colonisation in Kenya, which was taken up for distribution by roadshow man Dan Sonney. To spice it up, Sonney filmed his own "atrocity" footage – mostly topless black women being chased by men waving machetes and fake gore – and recut the film accordingly. The actual horrors of the Mau Mau far exceeded Sonney's contribution – at least 1,800 African civilians along with 200 British soldiers and policemen and 32 European settlers were killed, with many being tortured, mutilated, maimed and burned alive. Kenyan and British forces responded with equal brutality, including castrations and summary executions of militants. **Simba, Mark Of The Mau Mau** (1955), was a cheap British dramatization of events, with the militants being portrayed as terrorists and savages.

NIGHTMARE IN RED CHINA
Production: India/USA, 1954
Director: Shantaram Rajaram Vankudre/Lloyd Friedgen
Category: Atrocity
This roadshow atrocity film was originally **Dr. Kotnis Ki Amar Kahani**, a 1949 Hindi production directed by Shantaram, into which American producer Friedgen later inserted several crude sequences of nudity and violence; topless Asian women, the bayoneting of a priest, stabbings, medical experimentation and other blood-lettings convert what was formerly a romantic drama into a vile hybrid spectacle for slavering drunks of the night. Another Lloyd Friedgen film which preyed on fears of Communism was **Madmen Of Moscow** (1950), also a foreign film re-edited with added inserts.

DU RIFIFI CHEZ LES HOMMES
("A Clash Amongst Men")
Production: France, 1954
Director: Jules Dassin
Category: Crime/Heist

After making several hard-hitting film noirs, including **The Naked City** and **Brute Force**, director Dassin was forced to relocate to Paris after being victimized by the McCarthy witch-hunts. It was there that he made his masterpiece, **Du Rififi Chez Les Hommes**, the original heist-gone-wrong movie, showing how greed and mistrust after a jewel robbery lead to murderous violence; with its ensemble casting, 30-minute robbery sequence devoid of both dialogue and music, and its bleak, ineluctable aftermath, this was a blueprint for twisted crime films like Kubrick's **The Killing**, Giuliano Montaldo's **Ad Ogni Costo**, Mario Bava's atypical venture into crime **Rabid Dogs**, Ringo Lam's **City On Fire**, and right through to Tarantino's **Reservoir Dogs** and beyond.

WOMEN'S PRISON
Production: USA, 1954
Director: Lewis Seiler
Category: Women In Prison
A virtual remake of **Caged**, ramping up the sadism quotient and further delineating the genre's milieu of repressed sexuality, rebellion, humiliating punishments, and exaggerated stock characters ("new fish" to be corrupted, cruel sado-lesbian matron, "top dog" con, etc). Another variation on the prison theme – involving escape – came with Edward L. Cahn's **Betrayed Women** (1955), whose tag-line proclaimed: "Love-starved gun molls make a break for freedom!".

DOOMSTOWN USA
Production: USA, 1955
Category: Annihilation
Documentary footage from the US military of an atom bomb test carried out in the Nevada desert, and the damage sustained by an uninhabited town (peopled by mannequins) caught in the blast. The town is utterly destroyed, but most memorable are the scenes of the actual explosion and thermal shockwaves, the world transmogrified into a cataclysmic fireball of annihilation. Sometimes referred to as **"Survival Town" Atom Test**.

THE MAN WITH THE GOLDEN ARM
Production: USA, 1955
Director: Otto Preminger
Category: Drug Addiction
From the drug novel by Nelson Algren, the first big-budget Hollywood treatment of heroin addiction came in the wake of numerous cheap exploitation movies on a similar subject. As such, the film actually violated Industry Code regulations on the depiction of narcotics use; nevertheless, Frank Sinatra had signed up to star and, as a result, helped it escape the dreaded "condemned" rating which might have consigned it to the roadhouse circuit. This was a significant milestone in films in America being able to function without an industry seal of approval, and opened the door for other movies to depict drugs (and prostitution, and child birth) activity – which they quickly did in an ever-escalating deluge that irrevocably exploded in the 1960s. Preminger was a mainstream director who continued to cause controversy; his later courtroom drama **Anatomy Of A Murder** (1959) outraged many viewers by its moral ambiguity and use of terms such as "panties", "penetration", and "contraceptives", while he reportedly took LSD in preparation for the film which finally wrecked his career, the psychedelic screwball crime caper **Skidoo** (1968).

MONKEY ON THE BACK

Production: Canada, 1955-56
Director: Grant McLean/Julian Biggs
Category: Drugs Admonitory

Produced by the National Film Board of Canada, who had a geat reputation for supporting more avant-garde documentaries, this is an extremely bleak depiction of a heroin addict who loses everything because of his habit – wife, children, job, liberty, and finally his life when he ODs.

NIGHT OF THE HUNTER

Production: USA, 1955
Director: Charles Laughton
Category: Crime/Psychopath

Charles Laughton's one and only film as director is a flawed masterpiece, spoilt only by a hideously twee coda which somebody (surely not Laughton) tacked on. The film should really have ended with Preacher Harry Powell (Robert Mitchum) being hustled from the back of the jailhouse into a car and away to his date with the hangman (or, even better, with his actual lynching); as it stands, the film's whole tonal equilibrium is thrown out of kilter, its beautifully crafted horrors nullified. Up to that point, **Night Of The Hunter** forges a razor-fine balance between good and evil (the "right hand against the left"), its palette shifting from light into darkness and back again. Corrupt visions of sex, death and mendacity are pitted against the beauty of nature and the purity of children, though even the latter are fatally spiked (predation/cruelty, sexual awakening/vanity). Highlights are Mitchum's defining performance as the impotent, misogynistic, psychopathic pseudo-preacher Powell, with LOVE and HATE tattooed across his knuckles and a penis-substitute switchblade in his suit pocket, and scenes of exquisite visual poetry, such as a woman's submerged corpse, dressed in a white nightgown, throat slit, roped to a car at the bottom of a moonlit lake. A true crime, then, that the vile saccharine ending should undo such a mesmerising, often horrifying spell. **Night Of The Hunter** was based on a novel of the same name by Davis Grubb, which was in turn inspired by serial killer Harry Powers, "The Bluebeard of Quiet Dell", who was hanged in 1932 for his murders of two widows and three children.

NUIT ET BROUILLARD

("Night And Fog")
Production: France, 1955
Director: Alain Resnais
Category: Atrocity/War
Resnais' 30-minute documentary on Nazi war atrocities mixes archival photographs, newsreel, and shocking Signal Corps footage from the concentration camps with modern-day, colour sequences shot at the ruins of the most notorious camps. There is also a narration by a former inmate, and the film's implicit warning is one of a lingering evil poised to resurge at any given point in history.

THE PUSHER

Production: USA, c.1955
Director: Dwain Esper
Category: Drugs Admonitory
A late drugsploitation entry from Esper, combining footage from his 30s feature **Marihuana** with other drug-film clips and trailers, plus some newly-shot admonitory material. Shots of drug paraphernalia set the tone, and the pusher himself is played by Ed Wood regular Timothy Farrell, declaiming his agonized victims like some backstreet angel of death (footage most likely adapted from Merle W. Connell's 1949 sleaze-fest **The Devil's Sleep**). A production from Social Service Pictures, also responsible for the nudist film **They Wear No Clothes** (1956), amongst others, and not to be confused with **The Pusher** (1959), a fairly routine teenage drug movie from United Artists.

REBEL WITHOUT A CAUSE
Production: USA, 1955
Director: Nicolas Ray
Category: Juvenile Delinquency

The mainstream release of Nicolas Ray's **Rebel Without A Cause**, with its themes of teenage revolt, sexual confusion and doomed love, plus knife-fights and deadly car races, cemented the foundations of a new film genre, the JD (juvenile delinquent) movie. When the film's star, James Dean, died in a car wreck soon after the film's opening, another legend was born. Between them, Dean and the newly-risien music star Elvis Presley were the icons of a new youth movement, the rock and roll generation; but it was a movement instantly ripe for exploitation, a process which began that very same year with the release of **Blackboard Jungle**, another JD film whose theme song, "Rock Around The Clock" by Bill Haley, was already a sanitised version of the sexual threat offered by Presley. In 1956, AIP jumped on the bandwagon with **Hot Rod Girl**, the first of dozens of "wild youth" movies it would either produce or distribute over the following years.

THE BAD SEED
Production: USA, 1956
Director: Mervyn LeRoy
Category: Murder
From the play by Maxwell Anderson, about a murderous little girl who appears to be evil incarnate. Patty McCormack plays the psychotic child who kills anyone threatening to come between her and her idiot mother.

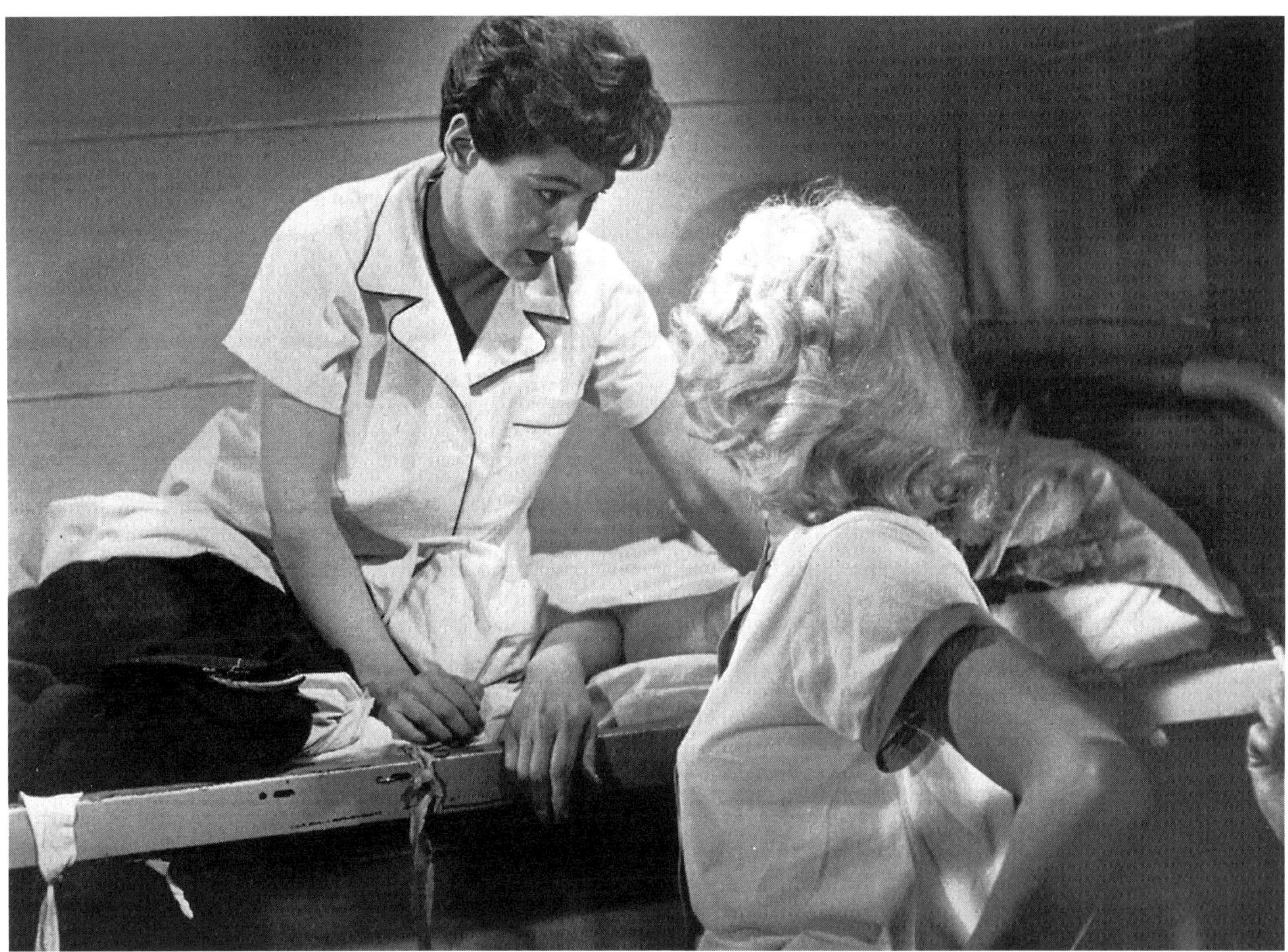

GIRLS IN PRISON
Production: USA, 1956
Director: Edward L. Cahn
Category: Women In Prison
Women's prison drama notable as being one of the first exploitation movies produced by the independent studio ARC, after changing their name to AIP (American International Pictures). AIP initially released **Girls In Prison** in a double bill with their own **Hot Rod Girl**, laying down not just the company's lucrative double-release strategy but also, more importantly, its trail-blazing new agenda of teenage delinquency, rock and roll culture, and girls gone bad. Another AIP prison movie of note was **Reform School Girl** (1957), but by 1960 and the release of the girl-on-Death-Row drama **Why Must I Die**, the WIP genre was running out steam, leaving the company to focus on other areas of teen activity (beach parties) and horror movies.

HOT ROD GIRL
Production: USA, 1956
Director: Leslie H. Martinson
Category: Juvenile Delinquency

"Teenage terrorists on a speed-crazy rampage!" Chicken-runs and teen angst at 100mph, this was the first in the 50s movie craze for hot rods, drag racing, rock and roll, and all-round juvenile delinquency. Distributed mainly by AIP, but also others like Allied Artists, these films celebrate teen hoodlums and rockers living on the edge – the edge of society, the edge of the law, the edge of death. The title **Hot Rod Girl** refers to the type of jailbait minx who used to hang around illegal drag-racers, a speed/danger groupie. Martinson followed up with **Hot Rod Rumble** (1957), another blast of murderous dragstrip action. Other entries in the sub-genre came thick and fast: **Drag Strip Girl** (1957), **Teenage Thunder** (1957), **Dragstrip Riot** (1958, featuring clashes between drag-racers and bikers, plus cult "bad girl" actress Yvonne Lime), **Hot Rod Gang** (1958, with an appearance by archetypal leather rocker Gene Vincent), **Joy Ride** (1958), **The Hot Angel** (1958), **Hot Car Girl** (1958), **Young And Wild** (1958, joy-riding), **Girls Town** (1959), and **Speed Crazy** (1959, featuring Yvonne Lime). Finally, when AIP came out with the mixed-genre **Ghost Of Dragstrip Hollow** in 1959, it was a signal that the hot rod movie craze had burned itself out, almost as quickly as it had flared up.

SWAMP WOMEN
Production: USA, 1956
Director: Roger Corman
Category: Female Delinquents/Exploitation
Corman's tale of three escaped female criminals hunting for stolen loot in a swamp borders on exploitation with scenes of alligator attacks, skimpy clothing and cat-fights. Another notable swamp movie was Harold Daniels' jailbait redneck lust triangle drama **Bayou** (1957), which after a poor first run was re-edited in 1961 by its producer, the roadshow denizen M.A. Ripps. Ripps cut in a rape scene (off-camera) and extra violence, retitled it **Poor White Trash** and succesfully relaunched it on the drive-in circuit, where it double-billed for many years with **I Hate Your Guts** (an alternative title for Roger Corman's **The Intruder**). Ripps had a penchant for the swamps and similar southern locations; he also produced **Macumba Love** and **Common Law Wife,** and acted as presenter for Carl K. Hittleman's **Big Daddy**, a bayou/alligators/voodoo/lust combo shot in 1965 and finally vented in 1969.

TAIYO NO KISETSU
("Season Of The Sun")
Production: Japan, 1956
Director: Takumi Furukawa
Category: Juvenile Delinquency
Film adaptation, by Nikkatsu Studios, of the sensational short first novel *Taiyo no Kisetsu* by Shintaro Ishihara, a young author who received one of the more coveted Japanese literary prizes, the Akutagawa Award, for his violent, adolescent outcry against tradition and the older generation. The book and film spawned the generic term *taiyozoku* ("sun tribe" or "teenage rebel") to describe this culture of teenage revolt, and a new youth movement was born. More *taiyozoku* films followed in quick succession, including **Shokei No Heya**, again from an Ishihara novel, and Ko Nakahira's nihilistic **Kurutta Kajitsu**, from an original Ishihara screenplay. While the controversial success of these movies paved the way for more and more exploitation titles, as Japanese cinema (reluctantly) became increasingly permissive, they also gave inspiration to a new generation of young film-makers like Nagisa Oshima and Kon Ichikawa, who would soon inaugurate the New Wave of Nippon cinema.

THE VIOLENT YEARS
Production: USA, 1956
Director: Ed Wood Jr.
Category: Girl Gangs/Crime

YIELD TO THE NIGHT
Production: UK, 1956
Director: J. Lee Thompson
US release title: **Blonde Sinner**
Category: True Crime/Execution

Ruth Ellis entered criminal history in 1955 when she became the last woman to be hanged in England. Peroxide blonde Ellis had shot dead her lover, failed racing-driver David Blakely, pumping four bullets into him outside the Magdala pub in Hampstead. **Yield To The Night**, starring the blonde bombshell of British cinema, Diana Dors, examines the case and the general reaction of horror and revulsion to the Ellis execution. Dors gives her best performance as the condemned woman, living out her last days in a tiny prison cell. A powerful, claustrophobic cry against capital punishment. Other British women's prison films of the period include **The Weak And The Wicked** (1954), Hammer's **Women Without Men** (1956) and **So Evil, So Young** (1961), but despite their exploitative titles, all are fairly tame

KILLER APE
Production: USA, 1953
Director: Spencer Gordon Bennet
Category: Jungle Fantasy/Science Fiction

MYTH

JUNGLE JIM IN PYGMY ISLAND
Production: USA, 1950
Director: William Berke
Category: Jungle Fantasy/Freak Film
After playing Tarzan for the last time, Johnny Weissmuller went to playing another jungle denizen, this time an adventurer in a safari suit. From 1948 to 1956 he played this character, Jungle Jim, in numerous movies and finally a TV series. The films were low-budget, often exploitative pulp; **Jungle Jim In Pygmy Island** is a prime example, using white dwarfs in black face and dressed up as tiny African natives in loincloths and bones. With cavorting dwarf actors Billy Barty, Angelo Rossitto and Billy Curtis, the film is a veritable freakshow unto itself, a gamut of ghastly shivers. Dwarfs were also used as pygmies in a later episode, **Jungle Moon Men** (1955). **Jungle Manhunt** (1951) used stock dinosaur footage from **One Million BC** and also used a man in costume to play one of the giant lizards, while the episode **Killer Ape** (1953) featured giant circus freak Max Palmer (standing at seven feet eight inches) as a monstrous caveman.

PREHISTORIC WOMEN
Production: USA, 1950
Director: Greg Tallas
Category: Fantasy

This film, along with W. Merle Connell's **Untamed Women** (1952), might be seen as forming a prototype for the concept of "girl gangs" in fantasy cinema, with narratives of primal females rampaging through ancient terrains or jungle settings, often fringing on sexploitation with skimpy costumes, cat-fights and other provocations. **Prehistoric Women** is also notable for featuring Johann Petursson, an eight-feet two-inch tall circus freak. Norman Dawn's **Bowanga Bowanga**, released in 1953, was another prime example of this trope, which continued through the decade with such entries as **She Gods Of Shark Reef** (1956), Curt Siodmak's **Love Slaves Of The Amazons** (1957), and the infamous **Wild Women Of Wongo** (1958). Any cursory reading of these narratives as "proto-feminist" is soon negated by their prime motive as exploitation, and resolutions which indicate wedding males as the solution to all worldly strife.

BOWANGA BOWANGA
Production: USA, 1951/54
Director: Norman Dawn
Alternative titles: **Bowanga Bowanga, White Sirens Of Africa; Wild Women.**
Category: Jungle Exploitation

JUNGLE MANHUNT
Production: USA, 1951
Director: Lew Landers
Category: Jungle Fantasy

ZWERG NASE
("Dwarf Nose")
Production: Germany, 1952
Director: Francesco Stefani
Category: Fairy-Tale/Freak Film
From a fairy tale by Wilhelm Hauff, written in 1826, this is the grotesque story of a young boy who is cursed by a witch and turns into a hideous dwarf with a huge long nose. The dwarf is played by Richard Krüger, who was also memorable playing evil, stunted and twisted characters in **Schneeweisschen Und Rosenrot** ("Little Snow-White And Rose-Red", 1955) and **Singende, Klingende Bäumchen** (1957), making a trilogy of blood-curdling freak horror shows which were somehow allowed to be watched by children. **Schneeweisschen Und Rosenrot** is among the most grotesque of all versions of Grimms' fairy-tales (this is not to be confused with the same *Snow White* story that Disney covered), featuring a truly malignant dwarf who is trying to rob two princes of their gold, one of whom he has transformed into a bear. With a

soundtrack of weird song snatches to compound its dark elements of freaks and shape-shifting, **Schneeweisschen Und Rosenrot** remains a wild haunting of the uncanny. **Zwerg Nase** director Francesco Stefani also oversaw **Singende, Klingende Bäumchen**, better-known in English as **The Singing, Ringing Tree**. Based on more stories by the Brothers Grimm, this was the bizarre tale of a prince who must deal with a hideous, evil dwarf in order to fetch his true love the prize she desires. The jerking, lurking dwarf (Krüger) is truly disturbing, pushing the film high up the ranks of freak film. Another frightening Grimms movie dwarf was Joseph Marz, who appeared in **The Magic Fountain** (1960).

JUNGLE JIM IN THE FORBIDDEN LAND
Production: USA, 1952
Director: Lew Landers
Category: Jungle Horror
One of the least-known of all beast-man movies, set in a hidden jungle populated by giant creatures who resemble werewolves. Director Landers previously supervised the vampire/werewolf tale **Return Of The Vampire**.

UNTAMED WOMEN
Production: USA, 1952
Director: W. Merle Connell
Category: Jungle Exploitation

SADKO
Production: USSR, 1952
Director: Aleksandr Ptushko
Category: Fantasy
One of the all-time classic Russian fantasy films, based on an ancient myth and set in medieval Ukraine and India. Costumes, sets, colours, lighting, effects and cinematography are all outstanding. This film was first released in the USA in a butchered, overdubbed and rescripted version entitled **The Magic Voyage Of Sinbad,** which bore limited resemblance to the original.

THE 5,000 FINGERS OF DR. T.
Production: USA, 1953
Director: Roy Rowland
Category: Fantasy

Specially written for the screen by Dr. Seuss (Theodor Geisel), **The 5,000 Fingers Of Dr. T.** is perhaps the wildest children's film ever produced by Hollywood; its expressionistic sets, dungeons and darker themes of adult cruelty and atom-age angst align it as much to **Son Of Frankenstein** as to **The Wizard Of Oz**. Essentially the nightmare of a dozing boy piano student, the film unfurls in the Dalíesque domain of Dr. T. himself, a piano teacher with 500 pupils, whose 5,000 fingers must play a concerto on a single, world's-largest grand piano. With ladders leading to nowhere, enigmatic holes and secret passageways patrolled by bizarre guards including Siamese twin child-catchers joined at the beard, Seuss's cinematic vision was unique at the time and remains unsurpassed, even by later, big-budget adaptations of his own books.

EL ENMASCARADO DE PLATA
("The Man In The Silver Mask")
Production: Mexico, 1953
Director: René Cardona
Category: Masked Crime-Fighter

This film is regarded as the first in Mexico's notorious masked wrestler-superhero genre, which would rise to predominate popular cinema in that country in the late 50s and throughout the 60s. The film was originally conceived as a starring vehicle for El Santo (Rodolfo Guzmán Huerta), the silver-masked *luchador* (wrestling star), who had recently risen to national celebrity by beating and unmasking one of his main rivals, Black Shadow, in the ring. When Santo declined, possibly due to fear of failure, the producers brought in another *luchador*, El Medico Asesino, who had already appeared in what technically stands as the country's first wrestling/crime movie, **Huracán Ramírez** (1952). In **El Enmascarado De Plata**, Medico Asesino plays a crime-fighter pitched against masked villains and hoodlums. El Santo was finally tempted into film a few years later, by fellow wrestler Fernando Osés, playing support roles in **El Cerebro Del Mal** and **Hombres Infernales** (both 1958), but his movie career really took off in 1961, with the release of **Santo Contra Los Zombies**, which saw him in the starring role and set the tone of pulp horror which his future films would generally pursue.

UGETSU MONOGATARI
("Tales Of The Moon And Rain")
Production: Japan, 1953
Director: Kenji Mizoguchi
Category: Period Fantasy

SHICHININ NO SAMURAI
("Seven Samurai")
Production: Japan, 1954
Director: Akira Kurosawa
Category: Historical/Chambara
With a total running-time of 203 minutes, Kurosawa's epic of *chambara* ("swordplay") and honour in feudal Japan was one of several of his works which would inspire numerous subsequent films in the Western genre, ranging from the bland **The Magnificent Seven** to Sergio Leone's genre-transforming **Per Un Pugno Di Dollari.** The most entertaining of all may be another Japanese production, Yasuharu Hasebe's **Sengoku Rokku Hayate No Onnatachi** (1974), in which a period rampage by seven sexy female mercenaries engenders plentiful nudity, sadism and sexual violence.

THE ADVENTURES OF CAPTAIN AFRICA
Production: USA, 1955
Director: Spencer Gordon Bennet
Category: Jungle Fantasy

A 15-chapter sequel to Columbia's 1943 serial **The Phantom** was initiated in 1955 by producer Sam Katzman, but changed to **The Adventures Of Captain Africa** when it was discovered that Columbia no longer held film rights to the original character. The result was an exceptionally cheap product, compiled largely from stock footage and containing four "recap" flashback chapters. It would be the company's final jungle serial. The chapters were: 1. **Mystery Man Of The Jungle!**; 2. **Captain Africa To The Rescue!**; 3. **Midnight Attack**; 4. **Into The Crocodile Pit!**; 5. **Jungle War Drums!**; 6. **Slave Traders!**; 7. **Saved By Captain Africa!**; 8. **The Bridge In The Sky!**; 9. **Blasted By Captain Africa!**; 10. **The Vanishing Princess!**; 11. **The Tunnel Of Terror!**; 12. **Fangs Of The Beast!**; 13. **Renegades At Bay!**; 14. **Captain Africa And The Wolf Dog!**; 15. **Captain Africa's Final Move!**.

DON QUIXOTE
Production: Spain, 1955-69
Director: Orson Welles
Category: Fantasy
One of Welles' great unreleased movies. Using his own money, the director began shooting it in Spain around 1955 and, between his many other activities, continued shooting bits and pieces for the next few years. He reportedly edited numerous sequences, and possibly multiple potential versions of the picture, but never completed final editing or post-production on a cut he considered definitive. Future sexploitation director Jésus Franco has a writing credit; he would later be assistant director on Welles' **Chimes At Midnight**.

JUNGLE MOON MEN
Production: USA, 1955
Director: Lew Landers
Category: Jungle Fantasy/Freak Film

PANTHER GIRL OF THE KONGO
Production: USA, 1955
Director: Franklin Adreon
Category: Jungle Horror/Science Fiction
Footage from Republic's 1941 serial **Jungle Girl** was first recycled in Republic's notoriously cheap feature **Daughter Of The Jungle** (1948), which starred Lois Hall as Ticoora, a white jungle queen, and then again in the company's penultimate serial, the 12-episode **Panther Girl Of The Kongo,** a jungle horror with a mad scientist who creates a mutant breed of giant "claw monsters". The serial's chapters were: 1. **The Claw Monster**; 2. **Jungle Ambush**; 3. **The Killer Beast**; 4. **Sands Of Doom**; 5. **Test Of Terror**; 6. **High Peril**; 7. **Double Trap**; 8. **Crater Of Flame**; 9. **River Of Death**; 10. **Blasted Evidence**; 11. **Double Danger**; 12. **House Of Doom.**

THE BEAST OF HOLLOW MOUNTAIN
Production: USA, 1956
Director: Edward Nassour, Ismael Rodríguez
Category: Fantasy Western

From an original story first conceived by stop-motion animator Willis O'Brien back in the 1930s and titled *The Valley Of The Mist*, **The Beast Of Hollow Mountain** was the first dinosaur western, concerning a rampaging Allosaurus in old Mexico. O'Brien's own script would eventually be shot in 1968, under the title **The Valley Of Gwangi**, with animation by Ray Harryhausen. **The Valley Of Gwangi**, directed by Jim O'Connelly, boasts superior monsters, and also an appearance by dwarf José Burgos as part of a travelling carnival. A carnival also features in another fantasy western of note, George Pal's **7 Faces Of Dr. Lao** (1963), in which Tony Randall appears as a snake-haired Medusa, the Great God Pan, the Abominable Snowman and other fabled man-beasts, while elements of SF and horror mark another weird western of the time, Jacques Marquette's **Teenage Monster** (1958).

THE THING FROM ANOTHER WORLD
Production: USA, 1951
Director: Christian Nyby
Category: Science Fiction

SCI-FI

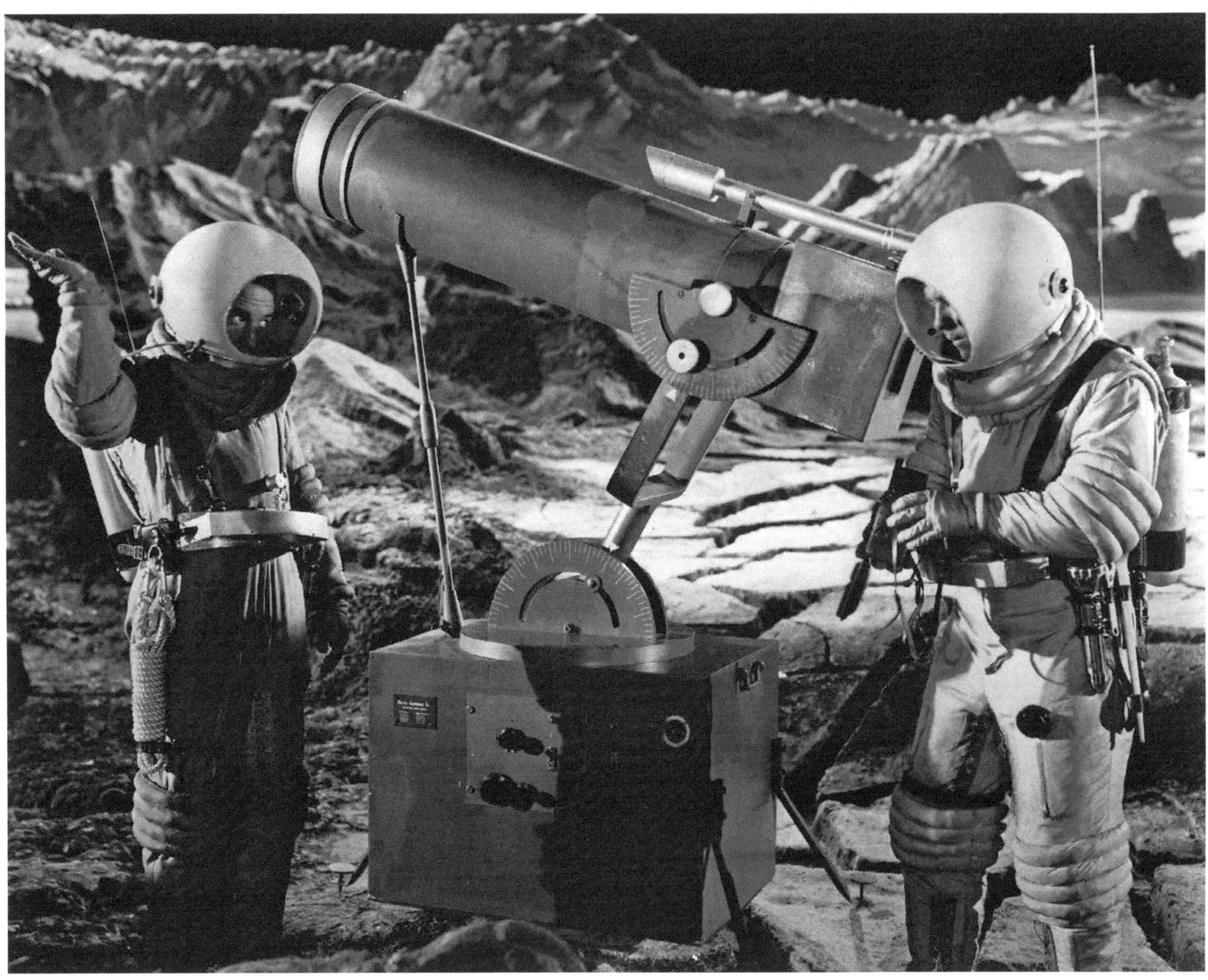

DESTINATION MOON
Production: USA, 1950
Director: Irving Pichel
Category: Science Fiction

Shot mainly in November and December 1949 under the working title **Operation Moon, Destination Moon** was one of the most technically plausible film depictions of space travel to that point. Produced by George Pal and co-scripted by Robert A. Heinlein (utilizing plot elements from his novel *Rocket Ship Galileo* and short story "The Man Who Sold The Moon"), the film's extensive pre-production research is reflected in its special effects (including stop-frame animation), hardware and lunar settings. Communist paranoia and atomic energy both figure in the storyline, as American scientists strive to construct a nuclear-powered rocket which will take them to the moon before the Soviets get there and use it as a missile base. Several plot elements – including using an oxygen tank as propellent to rescue an astronaut adrift in space, and the spaceship being too heavy or under-fuelled to return home with all its crew – were soon established staples in the SF film genre which **Destination Moon** helped to launch and define. The "space-race" genre was now underway, with entries such as Kurt Neumann's **Rocketship X-M** soon following.

ROCKETSHIP X-M
Production: USA, 1950
Director: Kurt Neumann
Category: Science Fiction

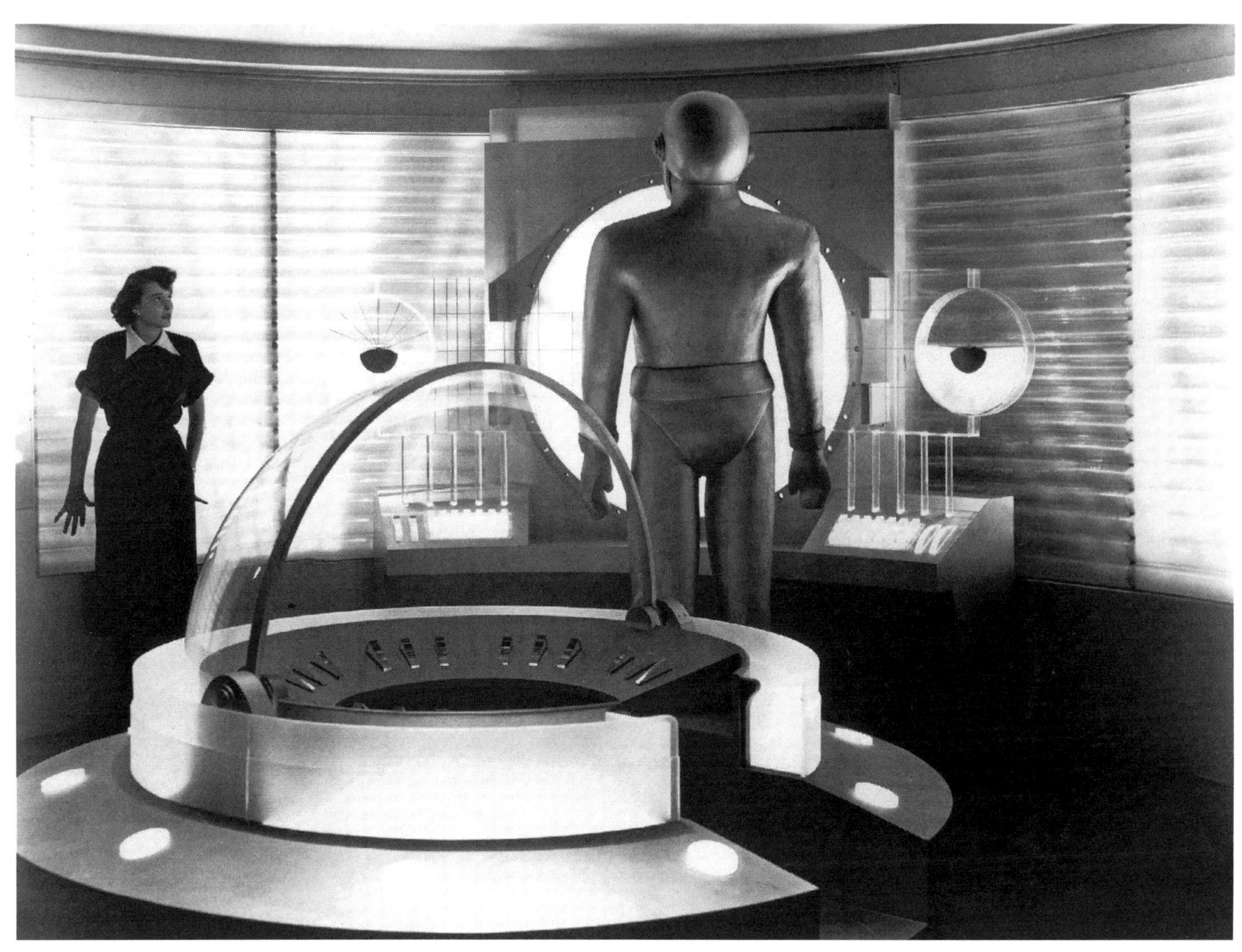

THE DAY THE EARTH STOOD STILL
Production: USA, 1951
Director: Robert Wise
Category: Science Fiction

FIVE
Production: USA, 1951
Director: Arch Obler
Category: Science Fiction
The first post-Hiroshima film to investigate a possible doomsday scenario in which all life on Earth has been wiped out by atomic war – except, in this case, for five survivors. This is a minimalist film, set mostly in a still-standing cliff-house (designed by Frank Lloyd Wright), with the odd foray into a corpse-strewn ghost city, and focusing on the interplay between the characters. Bleak and pessimistic, setting the tone for 50s SF whose main tropes were nuclear devastation, attack by giant insects, and invasion by genocidal space aliens.

THE MAN FROM PLANET X
Production: USA, 1951
Director: Edgar G. Ulmer
Category: Science Fiction

CAPTIVE WOMEN
Production: USA, 1952
Director: Stuart Gilmore
Category: Science Fiction
Not some women-in-prison entry, as the misleading title would suggest, but actually an innovative SF movie, probably the first post-apocalypse film to introduce the plot device of warring tribes striving for dominance in a nuclear wasteland; here the tribes are called The Norms, The Mutates, and The Upriver People (who have turned from worshipping God to worshipping Satan). This scenario would be replayed many times in subsequent genre outings, but this is where it originated.

RADAR MEN FROM THE MOON
Production: USA, 1951-52
Director: Fred C. Bannon
Category: Serial/Science Fiction
A 12-chapter Republic serial, introducing the character of Commander Cody as a rocket-powered space scientist. Cody would return in a second serial, **Commando Cody: Sky Marshal Of The Universe** (1953), which was originally planned as a television series. The episodes of **Radar Men From The Moon** were: 1. **Moon Rocket**; 2. **Molten Terror**; 3. **Bridge Of Death**; 4. **Flight To Destruction**; 5. **Murder Car**; 6. **Hills Of Death**; 7. **Camouflaged Destruction**; 8. **The Enemy Planet**; 9. **Battle In The Stratosphere**; 10. **Mass Execution**; 11. **Planned Pursuit**; 12. **Death Of The Moon Man.**

ZOMBIES OF THE STRATOSPHERE
Production: USA, 1952
Director: Fred C. Bannon
Category: Serial/Science Fiction
A 12-chapter Republic serial, originally planned as a sequel to **Radar Men From The Moon.** The chapters were: 1. **The Zombie Vanguard**; 2. **Battle Of The Rockets**; 3. **Undersea Agents**; 4. **Contraband Cargo**; 5. **The Iron Executioner**; 6. **Murder Mine**; 7. **Death On The Waterfront**; 8. **Hostage For Murder**; 9. **The Human Torpedo**; 10. **Flying Gas Chamber**; 11. **Man Vs. Monster**; 12. **Tomb Of The Traitors**. A condensed feature version, **Satan's Satellites**, was released in 1958.

CAT WOMEN OF THE MOON
Production: USA, 1953
Director: Arthur Hilton
Category: Science Fiction
A gold prospector on the Moon is assailed by nubile alien women in black tights and a giant space spider. Remade by Richard E. Cunha in 1959 as **Missile To The Moon.**

THE CREATURE FROM THE BLACK LAGOON
Production: USA, 1953-54
Director: Jack Arnold
Category: Science Fiction/Horror
A 3-D horror movie, Universal's last attempt at creating a new iconic monster to add to their impressive roster. Played by swimming ace Ricou Browning, the prehistoric beast-fish-man (or gill-man) is aroused from the depths of a South American lagoon by scientists, who attempt to capture it and take it back to civilization to be studied. The primal creature proves to be both violent and libidinous, killing some of its captors and abducting the sexy female team-member. Two sequels followed, **Revenge Of The Creature** (1955) and **The Creature Walks Among Us** (1956). A low-budget spin on the "gill-man" appeared in the Mexican production **El Pantano De Las Ánimas** ("Swamp Of Souls", 1957).

DONOVAN'S BRAIN
Production: USA, 1953
Director: Felix E. Feist
Category: Science Fiction/Horror

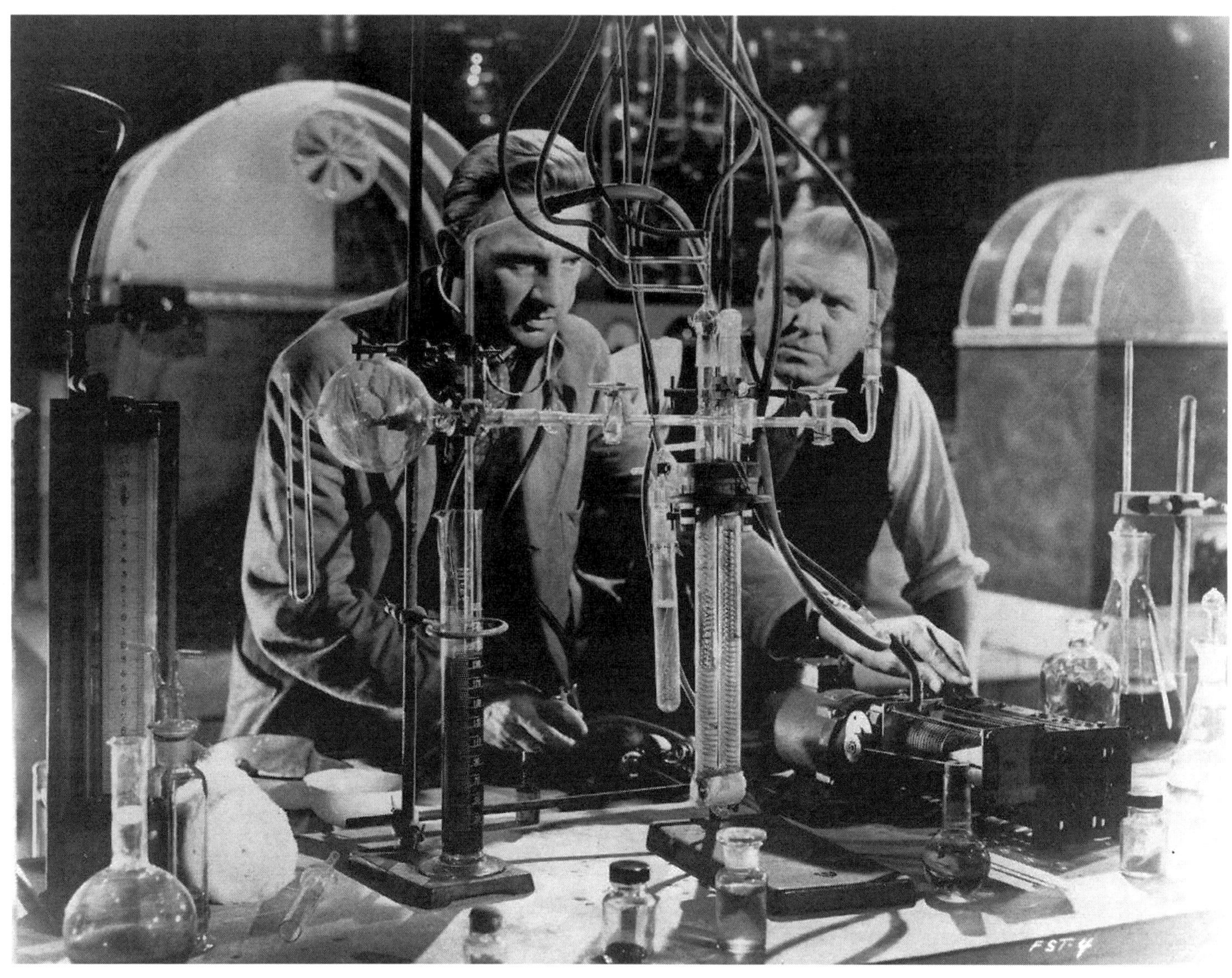

FOUR SIDED TRIANGLE
Production: UK, 1953
Director: Terence Fisher
Category: Science Fiction
Four-Sided Triangle, a Hammer Films co-production with Alexander Paal, deserves mention as Hammer's first venture into fantasy and science fiction (although its idea of duplicating a woman to make up for the loss of the original had already been tried in the company's **Stolen Face** [1952]). Here the scientific aspects were emphasised to such a degree that, as with many other SF pictures, these became the main point of appeal and "stars" could be largely dispensed with, allowing the money to be invested in sets and laboratory paraphernalia. Two scientists working in a barn in a remote village both fall in love with the same girl. She elects to marry one, leaving the other to overcome his grief by perfecting a machine to duplicate her exactly. Such is his success, however, that his reconstruction also prefers his romantic rival! Ultimately creator and creation perish in a laboratory fire.

INVADERS FROM MARS
Production: USA, 1953
Director: William Cameron Menzies
Category: Science Fiction

IT CAME FROM OUTER SPACE
Production: USA, 1953
Director: Jack Arnold
Category: Science Fiction

SPACEWAYS
Production: UK, 1953
Director: Terence Fisher
Category: Science Fiction
Hammer Films came up with **Spaceways** in an attempt to make a British picture to cash in on the post-war Hollywood "space exploration" cycle that had included **Rocketship X-M** (1950) and **Destination Moon** (1950). The space aspect provided an ingenious twist to a basic crime story with Howard Duff as the space scientist who is accused of having killed his wife and her lover and placed their bodies in an experimental satellite that will circle the earth until long after he is dead. To clear his name, the scientist goes up in a rocket to recover the satellite.

WAR OF THE WORLDS
Production: USA, 1953
Director: Byron Haskin
Category: Science Fiction

DEVIL GIRL FROM MARS
Production: UK, 1954
Director: David McDonald
Category: Science Fiction
As the trashy title suggests, this British SF film was the brainchild of American pulp producers – the Danzigers, who came to England in the early 1950s.

GOJIRA
Production: Japan, 1954
Director: Honda Ishiro
Category: Science Fiction/Daikaiju

The Japanese *daikaiju eiga* ("giant monster movies") – of which **Gojira** is the progenitor – are vehicles by which the devastation of Japan by earthquake, and the destruction of its cities by thermo-nuclear attack, can be re-enacted and rationalized as "nature's revenge", a response to man's mistreatment of the planet. In this way the movies, while superficially pure trash, actually carry a high mythic load as well as resonating with prescient allusions to modern-day chaos theory. **Gojira**, in which a gigantic radiocative reptilian threatens to annihilate Tokyo, was directed by Ishiro Honda, the doyen of Japanese pulp SF cinema, and he followed up not only with direct sequels – starting with **Gojira No Gyakushu** ("Gojira's Counter-Attack") in 1955 – but also films (all produced by Toho Studios) about other monstrous creatures including **Sora No Daikaiju Radon** ("Sky-Monster Radon", 1956), **Daikaiju Baran** ("Giant Monster Baran", 1958), Mothra (**Mosura**, 1961), and **San Daikaiju: Chikyu Saidai No Kessen** ("Three Giant Monsters: Greatest Battle On Earth", 1964). As well as starting the *daikaiju eiga* craze, **Gojira** also contains elements which would come to characterise the *tokusatsu* (special effects/masked superhero) genre, including the use of men in monster suits (*suitmation*) and miniature sets. Rival Daiei Studios tried to enter the *daikaiju* market in 1965 with **Daikaiju Gamera** ("Giant Monster Gamera"), a huge prehistoric fire-breathing turtle, whilst Toei Studios produced the bizarre *ninja/kaiju* hybrid **Kairyu Daikessen** ("Dragon-Monster Mega-Battle", 1966, released in the USA by AIP-TV as **The Magic Serpent**), about two mystic warriors with the power to transform into huge saurian beasts. The genre peak came in 1968 with Honda's **Kaiju Soshingeki** ("Total Monster Attack"), in which aliens seek to control all of the Toho creatures at the same time in order to subjugate the Earth. Like many Japanese SF films of the 50s and 60s, **Gojira** and its many successors were re-edited for US release with the inclusion of new footage of American actors (most commonly the booze-blasted Nick Adams); the originals are considerably preferable.

KILLERS FROM SPACE
Production: USA, 1954
Director: W. Lee Wilder
Category: Science Fiction

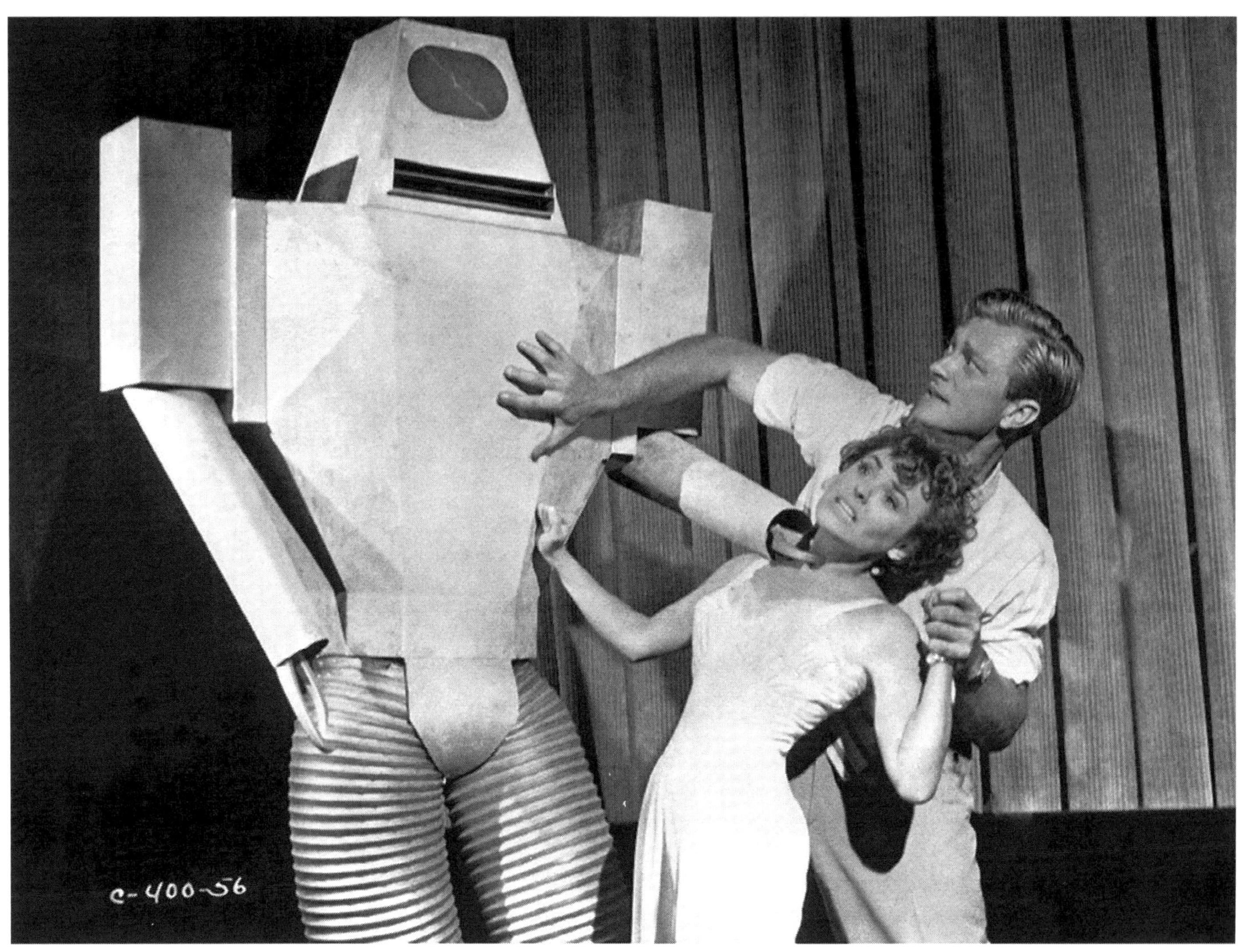

TARGET EARTH
Production: USA, 1954
Director: Sherman A. Rose
Category: Science Fiction

THEM!
Production: USA, 1954
Director: Gordon Douglas
Category: Science Fiction/Giant Bug

TOBOR THE GREAT
Production: USA, 1954
Director: Lee Sholem
Category: Science Fiction

20,000 LEAGUES UNDER THE SEA
Production: USA, 1954
Director: Richard Fleischer
Category: Science Fiction

THE BEAST WITH A MILLION EYES
Production: USA, 1955
Director: David Kramarsky & Lou Place
Category: Science Fiction/Horror
Executive produced by Roger Corman, this is the lowest of low-budget SF, but has some interesting ideas. An alien intelligence has landed in the Arizona desert and transferred its malevolence to all of the domestic animals in the area (hence the "million eyes", presumably). A retarded farm-worker also goes crazy before the alien is captured; its intelligence finally shifts to a desert rodent which is eaten alive by a heaven-sent bird of prey. Released on July 15, 1955, this was the first "horror" movie distributed by ARC (American Releasing Corporation), a company set up by James Nicholson and Samuel Z. Arkoff in 1954.

CONQUEST OF SPACE
Production: USA, 1955
Director: Byron Haskin
Category: Science Fiction

THE DAY THE WORLD ENDED
Production: USA, 1955
Director: Roger Corman
Category: Science Fiction/Horror
The first of several low-budget, high-imagination pulp SF movies directed by Corman in the latter 1950s. The film follows a group of survivors (including a burlesque stripper) after a nuclear holocaust, who are stalked by a hideous radiation-damaged mutant. An ARC release, originally on a double-bill with **The Phantom From 10,000 Leagues**. In April of the following year, ARC changed their name to AIP (American International Pictures), and entered into film production as well as distribution.

JUJIN YUKI OTOKO
("Beast Man, Snow Breed")
Production: Japan, 1955
Director: Ishiro Honda
US release title: **Half Human**
Category: Science Fiction

IT CAME FROM BENEATH THE SEA
Production: USA, 1955
Director: Robert Gordon
Category: Science Fiction
A generally dull giant creature movie, immeasureably enlivened by the stop-motion animation effects of Ray Harryhausen, here working on his first feature film. Despite budget limitations which restricted his giant, atomically-mutated octopus to only six limbs, Harryhausen produces great sequences of a hideous xenomorph from the depths. The only problem is the rest of the film. Harryhausen's next SF project would be **20 Million Miles To Earth**, for which he created the Ymir, a gigantic lizard-like alien from Venus.

THE QUATERMASS X-PERIMENT
Production: UK, 1955
Director: Val Guest
US release title: **The Creeping Unknown**
Category: Science Fiction/Horror

Following tentative explorations into science-fiction with **Four-Sided Triangle** and **Spaceways**, Hammer films produced their first fully-flegdged SF movie, **The Quatermass X-periment**, in 1955. It was derived from Nigel Kneale's sensationally successful British TV serial of July-August 1953, with the spelling of the word “Experiment” adjusted to emphasise the film's adults-only certificate (in America the film was retitled **The Creeping Unknown** by United Artists). Val Guest's direction and adaptation, with American writer Richard Landau, preserved much of the quality of the original. Brian Donlevy played Professor Quatermass, the man who has put Britain's first rocketship in space and investigates the disappearance of two of the crewmen on its return, together with the mysterious changes that have affected the only visible survivor. Richard Wordsworth gave a convincing portrayal of the latter figure, slowly succumbing to the alien force that possesses him and transforms him into a deformed monster which, in the tense climax, is electrocuted in the bowels of Westminster Abbey.

TARANTULA
Production: USA, 1955
Director: Jack Arnold
Category: Science Fiction/Horror

THIS ISLAND EARTH
Production: USA, 1955
Director: Joseph M. Newman
Category: Science Fiction

TIMESLIP
Production: UK, 1955
Director: Ken Hughes
US release title: **The Atomic Man**
Category: Science Fiction
A more sombre variant on the "atomic mutation" theme prevalent in the 1950s; a nuclear scientist accidentally saturated by radiation develops the ability to see seven seconds into the immediate future. He is inevitably pursued by gangsters, eager to exploit this potentially lucrative prescience.

-39

EARTH VS THE FLYING SAUCERS
Production: USA, 1956
Director: Fred F. Sears
Category: Science Fiction
A classic low-budget space alien invasion film, one of many made during this period when fear of Communism and other "outside" forces were at near-hysterical levels. Ray Harryhausen's stop-motion effects are less effective when applied to buildings and spacecraft than they are when used to animate creatures, but still provide a bizarre visual effect which adds to the film's deranged charms. Despite its budgetary restrictions, **Earth Vs The Flying Saucers** remains one of the definitive "alien invasion" movies of the 1950s, along with more bigger-budget others like **The Day The Earth Stood Still**.

FIRE MAIDENS FROM OUTER SPACE
Production: UK, 1956
Director: Cy Roth
Category: Science Fiction
Low-budget British SF fantasy, with astronauts landing on a moon of Jupiter and encountering hordes of scantily-clad young women, the slaves of a man descended from Atlantis. A mutant creature also lurks in the shadows as the women try to seduce the visitors into mating and breeding with them.

FORBIDDEN PLANET
Production: USA, 1956
Director: Fred M. Wilcox
Category: Science Fiction

INVASION OF THE BODY SNATCHERS
Production: USA, 1956
Director: Don Siegel
Category: Science Fiction

1824-1 AD

THE MOLE PEOPLE
Production: USA, 1956
Director:Virgil W. Vogel
Category: Science Fiction

THE WEREWOLF
Production: USA, 1956
Director: Fred F. Sears
Category: Science Fiction/Horror
Luminously photographed in haunting nocturnal snowscapes, **The Werewolf** is one of the best of the low-budget lycanthropy movies. Director Sears applies the visual hallmarks of film noir to the story, which avoids the usual supernatural elements in favour of a scientific explanation; the lycanthrope is an amnesiac, the victim of two doctors who inoculated him with an overdose of an experimental serum, designed to prevent radiation sickness. As a result, he mutates into a fercious wolf-creature when faced with aggression. Only those who threaten him die; a mugger, the two doctors seeking to euthanize him to cover their crime, all are ripped to shreds. In the end, the man is gunned down whilst crossing a bleak promontory, and his "curse" is laid to rest. An unusual angle on the 1950s nuclear paranoia movie.

WORLD WITHOUT END
Production: USA, 1956
Director: Edward Bernds
Category: Science Fiction

X... THE UNKNOWN
Production: UK, 1956
Director: Leslie Norman
Category: Science Fiction

X... The Unknown deals with a monstrous sludge which quietly slithers out of the ground following an earth tremor in a remote area of Scottish moorland and proceeds to eat up members of the local population; finally an atomic scientist, Dr Adam Royston (Hollywood's Dean Jagger) deduces that the thing is after radioactive material, and works out a way to corner it at an atomic research station and dispose of it. The film remains an interesting early example of the "shapeless monster" genre definitively explored in **The Blob** (1958), but by its contrasting bleakness and aura of despair manages to articulate a very real form of post-Atomic angst.

SOMMAREN MED MONIKA
("Summer With Monika")
Production: Sweden, 1953
Director: Ingmar Bergman
Category: Sex

SEX

UN CHANT D'AMOUR

("A Love Song")
Production: France, 1950
Director: Jean Genet
Category: Homo-Erotic

A poetic homosexual prison fantasy which was banned for its scenes of "hardcore pornography" (including erect penises), author Jean Genet's short film stands as a landmark in both underground cinema and homoerotic sub-culture. According to Violette Leduc, that same year Genet also made a 3-minute home movie at the home of arts patron Jacques Guérin. Genet apparently conceived of the sketch in which he plays a baby whipping his hapless mother (Leduc) throughout a baptism ceremony. Genet's lover Java plays the baby's governess. Leduc comments that Genet – swathed in a bed sheet and wearing a real baby's bonnet – looked like an earthworm in a bundle of linen. The film is now lost. Genet's subsequent engagement with cinema was disappointingly limited and fragmentary. In 1955, he contributed dialogue to Georges Lacombe's **La Lumiere En Face**, a tale of sexual abstinence leading to murder, but later asked his name to be removed from the credits. Similarly **L'Arrestation D'Un Tireur Des Toits** ("Arrest Of A Roof-Top Sniper"), a 1962 adaptation of Genet's homo-erotic novel *Funeral Rites*, was never released commercially after Genet again demanded his name be removed from the project. Meanwhile **Un Chant D'Amour** continued to grow in stature as a work of revolutionary cinema; the film has served as an inspiration to subsequent generations of film-makers of all sexual persuasions, perhaps as much as his writing.

DIE GÖTTIN VOM RIO BENI

("The Goddess Of Rio Beni")
Production: Brazil/Germany, 1950
Director: Franz Eichhorn
Alternative title: **Mundo Extrano**
US release title: **Strange World**
Category: Ethno-Documentary/Mondo

Commercially-released ethnographic documentaries or dramatizations had long been one of the main legitimate ways for audiences to look at naked females, and nothing changed in the 1950s. This adventure, filmed in the jungles of Brazil, stands as a precursor to the ethnosploitational "mondo" films of the 1960s, such as **Kwaheri**, in both its content and marketing (despite being fictional); posters for the film promise "the feared piranha fish devouring its prey", "anaconda, the world's largest snake, crushing it victim", "the fierce head-hunters of the Amazon in beserk frenzy", and "the secret rites of tribes untouched by civilization", and of course showed pictures of naked natives as well as white girls under threat of violation by savages.

LATUKO
Production: USA, 1950-52
Director: Edgar M. Queeny
Category: Ethno-Documentary/Mondo

The infamous case of the museum-sponsored educational film which got banned. Written by Charles L. Tedford, this film of Sudanese natives was commissioned by the American Museum of Natural History but fell foul of the law by displaying full-frontal genital nudity, even though it was in a (supposedly) innocent context; under New York State Law it was deemed both "immoral", and "likely to incite crime". Other disturbing scenes include blood-drinking, goat sacrifice and self-mutilatory rites, all relating to the coming of age of a young male. Edgar M. Queeny and Fort B. Guerin were the cinematographers.

THREE COMRADES
Production: USA, c.1950
Director: Anonymous
Category: Pornography/Queer

A pornographic stag reel, regarded as one of the the first exclusively homosexual (as opposed to man/woman/man or man/drag queen) film in that predominantly heterosexual market, showing three men engaged in mutual sodomy and fellatio. Visible homosexual cinema in the 50s and early 60s consisted solely of "beefcake" (muscular men posing in G-strings) and other seemingly inocuous activities which could be passed off as physical education.

THE WONDROUS STORY OF BIRTH
Production: USA/Canada, 1950
Director: Claude Alexander
Category: Gynaecology

Contraception, infertility treatments, venereal disease, pregnancy, childbirth – none of these subjects is remotely erotic, yet they served as sexploitation lures by thir association with the sexual act, and the opportunities they afforded for glimpses of female nudity and, in a few cases, genitalia. **The Wondrous Story Of Birth** must be one of the most lurid and unpleasant of all the roadshow childbirth reels, assembled by Alexander (a former employee of Kroger Babb) from various sources, and combined with a 1948 Canadian film called **The Sins Of The Fathers** to make a new package which he called **No Greater Sin**. The birth reel was also sold as a 20-minute item, combining black and white and colour footage, under the titles **The Birth Of Triplets** and **The Wondrous Story Of Birth**. The film itself contains such nauseating footage as a delivery using surgical forceps, a small vaginal opening being artificially enlarged with a scalpel, triplets removed from a woman's sliced-open belly (Caesarian Section), and even a penile circumcision, for good measure. Grotesque in every way, Alexander's film belongs to the nascent worldwide body of often prurient and sensationalistic documentaries which would eventually become known as "mondo".

HON DANSADE EN SOMMAR
("She Danced One Summer")
Production: Sweden, 1951
Director: Arne Mattsson
US release title: **One Summer Of Happiness**
Category: Sex
The first post-war film from Sweden with nude scenes (a young couple swimming together and embracing), an international hit which helped to establish the myth of Sweden as the country of free sex. Two years later came Ingmar Bergman's **Sommaren Med Monika**, with similar sexually-charged scenes, and the Swedish reputation was sealed – at least until films from Denmark helped usher in the golden age of hardcore, at the start of the 1970s. **Monika** found notoriety when it was picked up for distribution in 1955 by a young entrepreneur, David F. Friedman, then working for roadshow company Modern. Friedman edited and over-dubbed the original, and then spliced in extra nude scenes, for release under the title **Monica, The Story Of A Bad Girl**. Friedman would finally get his break as producer in the early 60s, when he teamed up with director Herschell Gordon Lewis for a series of low-budget hits. Another Swedish film from 1953 to suffer the American roadshow treatment was Hans Dahlin's **Ogift Fader Sökes**, a teenage pregnancy drama repackaged by President Films as **Unmarried Mothers** in 1956.

SMART ALEC
Production: USA, c.1951
Director: Anonymous
Category: Pornography
Well-known stag loop featuring stripper Candy Barr and oral sex. Legend has it that Barr, fifteen at the time, was drugged and coerced into making the film at gunpoint.

MAGIE VERDE
Production: Italy, 1952
Director: Gian Gaspare Napolitano
Category: Ethno-Documentary/Mondo
Among the first in a new breed of exotic documentaries produced in Italy during the 1950s, mixing fact with fictional aspects, and exploring/exploiting controversial subject matter and "secret" ethnographic mysteries; filmed records of travels throughout uncharted lands, recording aspects of magico-religious rituals as well as native nudity and lethal wildlife action such as snake attacks – a format which had been extant since the first decades of cinema, but which would now grow increasingly exteme in content. Next in this genre came such films as **Continente Perduto** ("Lost Continent", 1955) directed by Enrico Gras, Giorgio Moser and Leonardo Bonzi in Malaysia and Borneo, and **L'Impero Del Sole** ("Empire Of The Sun", Enrico Gras, 1955). These three films clearly laid the groundwork for the Italian "mondo" movies of the 1960s. The ethnographic theme was developed in the likes of Lionetto Fabbri's Malaysian documentary **Malesia Magica** (1961), which investigated prostitution in modern cities, but by that time other films in this emergent genre had already started to look closer to home for their subject matter.

TÖDLICHE LIEBE
("Deadly Love")
Production: Germany, 1952-53
Alternative title: **Tabus Der Sexualität**
Director: Fred Barius
Category: Sex Education
Known as **Erotikens Offer** in Sweden, where it was banned outright until 1965.

GLEN OR GLENDA
Production: USA, 1953
Director: Ed Wood Jr.
Category: Transvestism/Sexploitation
Two sordid psychiatric tales of cross-dressing and hermaphroditism, with Bela Lugosi and Satan thrown in for good measure. A George Weiss production. Weiss, who reportedly wanted a film to cash in on the Christine Jorgensen sex-change case, added additional scenes of sexual violation and striptease to spice up Wood's finished film. Wood was largely engaged in the production of horror-type movies during the 1950s, but by the 60s had himself progressed to sexploitation and, eventually, pornography.

LUCRÈCE BORGIA
Production: France, 1953
Director: Christian-Jaque
Category: Historical/Sex
French historical films of the 1950s which dealt with lurid subject matter were sure to include as much female nudity as possible. and **Lucrèce Borgia**, starring Martine Carol in the title role, was no exception. Another example was Abel Gance's **La Tour de Nesle** (1954-55).

TEST TUBE BABIES
Production: USA, 1953
Director: W. Merle Connell
Category: Sexploitation
Sensationalistic dramatic treatment of artificial insemination. Reworked and retitled **The Pill** in 1968.

TOURBILLON
("Whirlwind")
Production: France, 1953
Director: Alfred Rode
Category: Sexploitation/Crime

THE VICE AND THE BADGE
Production: USA, c.1953
Director: Richard Fontaine
Category: Queer
Also known as **Beach Bar Nightmare**, this 16mm homoerotic loop was one of many produced by Fontaine's company Zenith, a pioneer in the field alongside Bob Mizer's AMG (Athletic Model Guild).

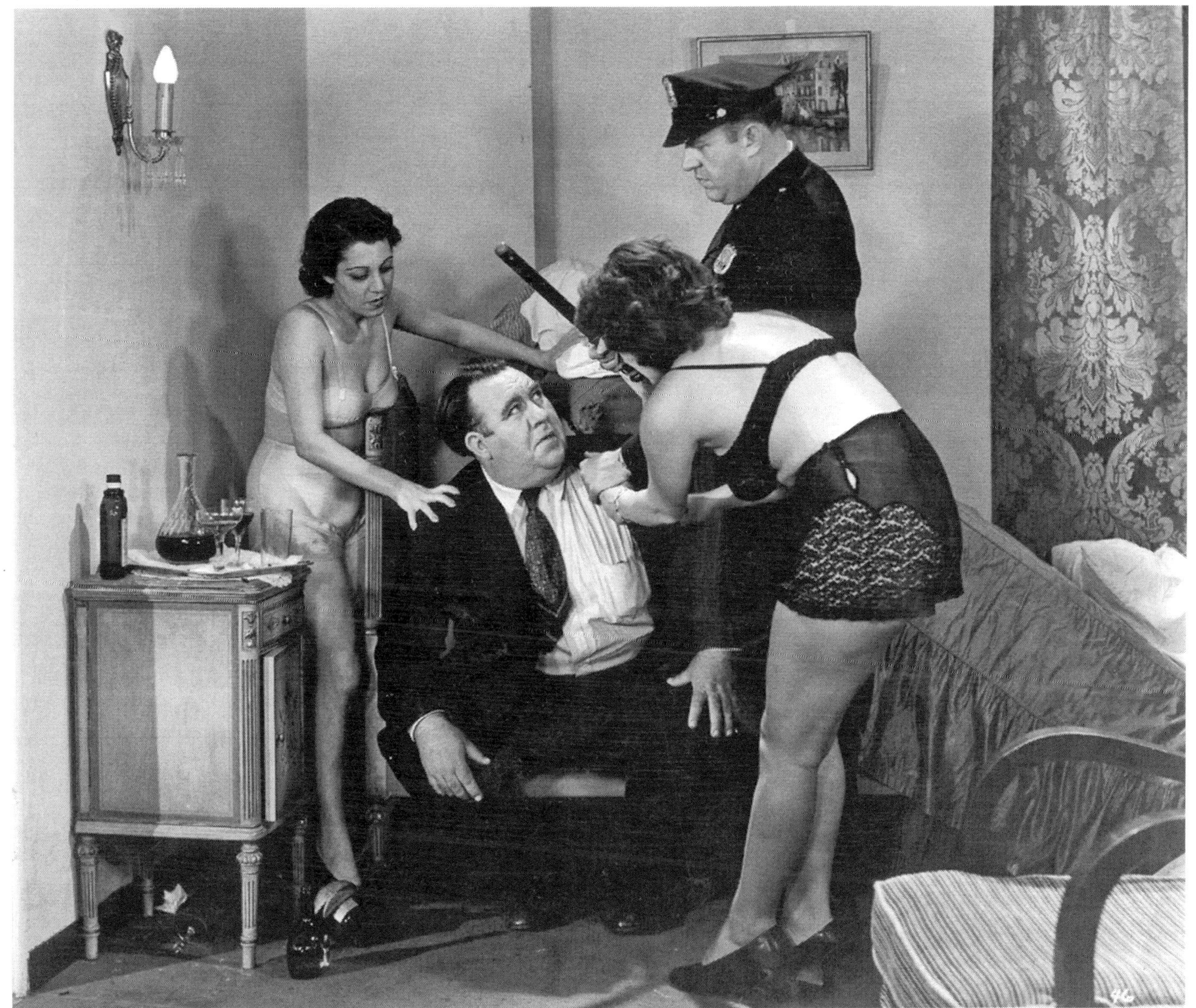

VIOLATED
Production: USA, 1953
Director: Walter Strate
Category: Sexploitation/Crime
Notable as the first film to be produced by (it was also written by) William Mishkin, a burlesque film promoter who went on to create a career in exploitation film production and, especially, distribution, **Violated** is a sex/crime amalgam concerning a serial killer who stalks, slaughters and semi-scalps his victims in various parts of New York City. There are strippers as well as murder scenes and atmospheric urban grime, and Mishkin tries to redeem the sleaze by ending with a psychoanalysis of the case. (Not to be confused with Kurt Neumann's **Violated** [1954], a white slavery flick set in Rio.) Mishkin next worked on several films with Jerald Intrator, financing the latter's skin-teasers **The Sexperts: Touched By Temptation** (1965) and **Caught In The Act!** (1966), before teaming up with the notorious Andy Milligan to make **The Promiscuous Sex** (1967), the first of numerous director-producer collaborations in a volatile working relationship extending into the 70s

AH! LES BELLES BACCHANTES...
("Ah! The Beautiful Debauchers...")
Production: France, 1954
Director: Jean Loubignac
Category: Sexploitation

FEITIÇO DO AMAZONAS
("Spell Of The Amazon")
Production: Brazil, 1954
Director: Zygmunt Sulistrowski
US release title: **Naked Amazon**
Category: Ethno-Documentary/Mondo

THE GARDEN OF EDEN
Production: USA, 1954
Director: Max Nosseck
Category: Nudism
Nosseck's film retains historically important for a 1957 court decision which ruled that onscreen nudity was not obscene, thereby opening the floodgates for a slew of similar films. Such incremental legal victories evenually led to the legalisation of pornography in the USA, in the late 1960s.

KARAMOJA
Production: USA, 1954
Director: William B. Treutle
Category: Mondo
A notoriously exploitative ethno-documentary, shot in Africa and featuring such tribal rites as blood and piss-drinking, animal dismemberment, mutilation, flesh-piercing, bathing in dung, and unanaethetized circumcision as well as the usual native nudity. A Kroger Babb presentation.

TIJUANA AFTER MIDNITE
Production: USA, 1954
Director: Phil Tucker
Category: Striptease
The most crude and basic form of entertainment, set in a sleazy backstreet nightclub with a succession of tame strip routines interspersed with boring stand-up comedy. Tucker also made the similar **Dance Hall Racket** (1953) and **Dream Follies** (1954, with Lenny Bruce). The Willis Kent production **Dreamland Capers** (1958) was an example of the same format. A lot more interesting and stimulating were the individual loops of strippers produced by numerous companies during this period for home projection, especially the "beast and beauty" acts involving a gorilla and a near-naked woman.

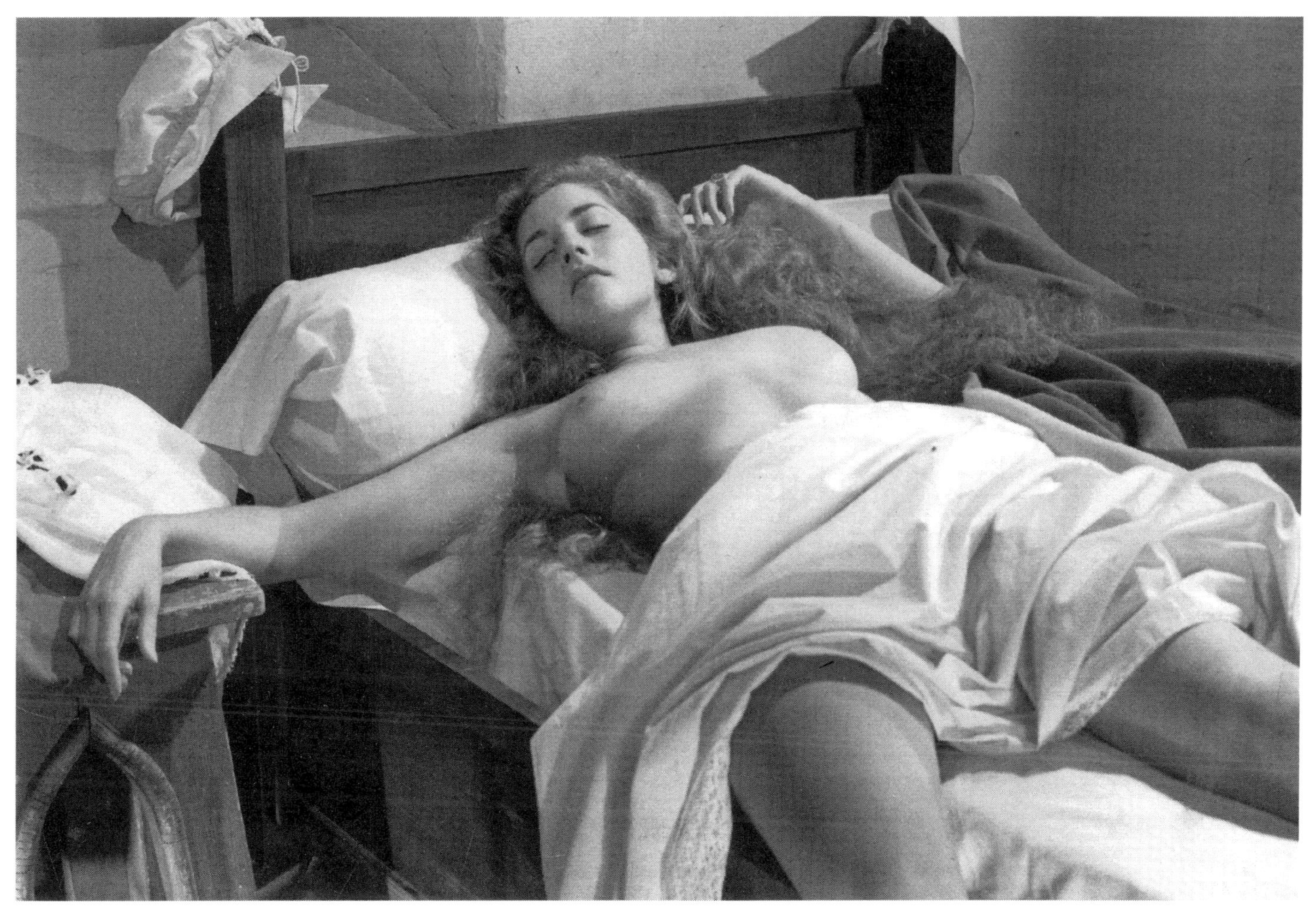

LA TOUR DE NESLE
("The Tower Of Nesle")
Production: France, 1954-55
Director: Abel Gance
Category: Historical/Sex
One of numerous film adaptations of Alexandre Dumas' historical novel *La Tour De Nesle*, in which he sensationalized events which occurred in 1314. At the centre of this historical scandal were King Philip IV of France and his daughter, Isabella. Isabella accused Philip's three daughters-in-law of committing adultery, with two knights, in the Tower of Nesle (a guard tower in the old city wall of Paris). These accusations led to a series of arrests, imprisonments, tortures and brutal executions; the knights were reportedly castrated, flayed alive, broken on the wheel, and hanged. As in the previous version of 1937, Gance depicts this hotbed of depravity with as much female nudity as permissible.

L'AFFAIRE DES POISONS
("The Poison Affair")
Production: France, 1955
Director: Henri Decoin
Category: Historical/Witchcraft

A prime example of the French *penchant* for decadent and lascivious recreations of historical events. 1670s Paris was a hotbed of Satanism, with the Black Mass (a modern version of the old Witches' Sabbat) being invented by the French witch La Voisin (burned alive in 1680). At the Black Mass – preferably held in a deserted or desecrated Christian church – obscene representations of the saints, the Virgin, and of the Son of Man were employed. In some cases the image of the Virgin, raddled and dissolute of mien, was equipped with breasts to be suckled, and with a vagina into which the penis might be inserted. In the case of the Christ-figures, there was sometimes a phallus, which Devil-worshippers both sucked and inserted into vagina or anus, depending upon the sex of the communicant. Occasionally, rather than an image, an actual human figure was bound to the cross and fulfilled the Christly role, eventually discharging his semen which was collected in a blasphemously consecrated chalice and used in the making of the Host. Semen, along with excreta and menstrual blood, was a standard ingredient of these Devil's hosts, which were converted by the saying of the appropriate words, into the Body of Our Lord. The Hosts were inserted into anus and vagina, urinated and defecated upon, smeared with semen, and finally consumed. La Voisin, with her abominable crew of sorceresses and corrupt priests, specialized in ceremonies to win back, or win over, lovers; this involved the client offering her naked body as an altar and a vehicle for various obscene acts. Perhaps the most famous client of La Voisin was the beautiful Marquise de Montespan, who requested a Black Mass where it was magically ordained that the Queen become barren, and cast out by King Louis XIV, and that Louis would take the Marquise for his lover. This all came to pass, but in 1673, when she feared she might be supplanted by a rival, the Marquise and La Voisin held another, more potent Mass. They summoned a Satanic defrocked priest – the sinister and hideously ugly Abbé de Guiborg, who pronounced no less than three black rites over the Marquise's naked and ritually sodomized body. It is said that the blood of a sacrificed child was used for the wine, and mixed with flour to make the Host. Finally an incantation was recited, calling on "Astaroth and Asmodeus, princes of amity" to grant Montespan's requests. In the end La Voisin resorted to poison, leading to an attempt on the King's life. When the King learned of all this, he was so shocked that he ordered all evidence of it suppressed. **L'Affaire Des Poisons** is a refreshingly lurid presentation of these events, and actress Danielle Darrieux as Montespan goes completely naked in the Black Mass scenes, which were shocking for their time in some countries.

CONTINENTE PERDUTO
("Lost Continent")
Prodction: Italy, 1955
Director: Enrico Gras, Giorgio Moser & Leonardo Bonzi
Category: Ethno-Documentary/Mondo

LA MÔME PIGALLE
("The Pigalle Girl")
Production: France, 1955
Director: Alfred Rode
Category: Red Light/Crime
Perhaps the best of a 1950s sub-genre of French cinema set in the sleazy Parisian nightclub world of Montmartre and Pigalle, featuring strippers, whores, pimps and crooks. These films were marked by scenes of topless female nudity and street slang, and often screened only in special matinées. In **La Môme Pigalle** (known in English as **The Maiden**), a dancer is murdered by her jealous boss. Foot fetishists will enjoy the scenes of star Claudine Depuis washing her dirty feet in the sink. Depuis, well-known for playing the role of stripper or slut, was married to director Rode. They worked together on a series of films, including **Boîte De Nuit** (1951) and **Tourbillon** (1953), the former being released by William Mishkin in the US as **Hotbed Of Sin**, in 1961.

SAMBA FANTÁSTICO
Production: Brazil/France, 1955
Director: Jean Manzon
Category: Ethno-Documentary/Mondo

SLASH OF THE KNIFE GOD
Production: USA, 1955
Director: Andy Dietz
Sub-title: **A Story Of The Green Trap**
Category: Jungle Exploitation
16mm short ethno-document, with staged scenes, detailing male circumcision amongst African natives and other jungle aberrations.

TEASERAMA
Production: USA, 1955
Director: Irving Klaw
Category: Burlesque/Striptease
Klaw, a notorious girlie photographer of the 50s, also made two short burlesque movie features that both starred his main model, the now world-famous pin-up Bettie Page (the other was **Varietease** in 1954). Other dancers in the films include Tempest Storm, Blaze Starr, Honey Baer, Vicki Lynn, and other 50s icons of tease. Klaw also made **Buxom Beautease** (1956), as well as dozens, probably hundreds, of short films of Bettie and the others in various situations; these break down roughly into three categories: fetish/bondage, burlesque/dancing, and catfight/wrestling. Although Klaw destroyed much of his work when he came under federal investigation, a significant amount still survives, affording a glimpse into a relatively innocent (there is no sex, no significant nudity) world that still has the power to arouse. Bettie Page also appeared in the burlesque feature **Striporama** (1953), directed by Jerald Intrator, and later can be glimpsed in the first Michael Findlay film, **Body Of A Female** (1964).

ADÁN Y EVA
Production: Mexico, 1956
Director: Alberto Gout
Category: Bible Exploitation
A daring biblical film with a near-naked Eve, which was soon picked up for roadshow distribution in the US by William Horne. A later Mexican variation, **El Pecado Se Adán Y Eva** ("The Sin Of Adam And Eve"), was made in 1969 and could therefore display much more abundant nudity, as well as scenes such as Adam wrestling with the snake Satan.

ET DIEU... CRÉA LA FEMME
("And God Created Woman")
Production: France, 1956
Director: Roger Vadim
Category: Sexy

Vadim's first film became a hit for one reason alone – Brigitte Bardot, and the glimpses afforded of her semi-naked, voluptuous body. One of the first "arthouse" films imported from Europe to America, where sex-starved patrons queued to see "legitimate" nudity – prompting US exploitation distributor DCA to acquire **En Effeuillant La Marguerite**, a 1956 comedy in which Bardot had a supporting role, and launch it in English as **Mademoiselle Striptease** (actually the title of another French film, made in 1957, with no Bardot).

LIANE, DAS MÄDCHEN AUS DEM URWALD
("Liane The Jungle Girl")
Production: Germany, 1956
Director: Eduard von Borsody
US release title: **Liane, Jungle Goddess**
Category: Sexploitation/Jungle
Among the first post-war films from Germany to feature white female nudity, this was basically a female version of *Tarzan* with a topless teenage actress (Marion Michael) prancing in the jungle with other topless (native) women. An adults-only hit which quickly spawned an inferior sequel, **Liane: Die Weisse Sklavin** ("Liane: The White Slave", 1957); the two films were later edited together as **Liane, Die Tochter Des Dschungels** ("Liane, Daughter Of The Jungle", 1961). **Liane** paved the way for a host of other, increasingly daring "teen sex symbol" films in Germany, such as the "white slavery" movies **Schwarze Nylons – Heisse Nächte** ("Black Nylons, Hot Nights", 1958) and **Das Nachtlokal Zum Silbermond** ("The Silver Moon Nightspot", 1959).

ONNA SHINJUO NO FUKUSHU
("Revenge Of The Pearl Woman")
Production: Japan, 1956
Director: Toshio Shimura
Category: Sexploitation/Crime
Although the semi-stag movie **Nikutai No Ichiba** (1962) is often regarded as the first "pink" (erotic) movie in Japanese cinema, glimpses of female anatomy were not uncommon even in the 1950s. One of the first actresses to appear nude was Yukiko Shimazaki, in Satsuo Yamamoto's **Hi No Hate** (1954), a left-wing independent film. The trend was sneakily initiated into more mainstream entertainment by Shintoho Studios with a new genre, the "girl diver" movie, commencing in 1956 with **Onna Shinjuo No Fukushu** which starred the curvy Michiko Maeda. Girls were shown wet-bloused, then later topless, then later even naked as they dived for pearls in such films as Shimura's **Ama No Senritsu** (1957) and **Ama No Bakemono Yashiki** (1959, released in the US as **Girl Divers Of Spook Mansion**). Katono Goro's **Kaidan Ama Yurei** (1960) continued this theme of sexy quasi-horror. Other studios took advantage of Shintoho's breakthrough to push the boundaries of screen nudity, and Nikkatsu's **Nikutai No Hanko** (1957) notoriously showed a woman absolutely naked climbing into bed, with a long erotic close-up of her hairy armpit.

INDEX OF MAIN ENTRIES

ADÁN Y EVA (1956) 128
THE ADVENTURES OF CAPTAIN AFRICA (1955) 66
L'AFFAIRE DES POISONS (1955) 120
AH! LES BELLES BACCHANTES... (1954) 116, 117
THE BAD SEED (1956) 48
THE BEAST OF HOLLOW MOUNTAIN (1956) 69
THE BEAST WITH A MILLION EYES (1955) 91
THE BIG HEAT (1953) 34
THE BLACK CASTLE (1952) 9
THE BLACK SLEEP (1956) 2, 22
BOWANGA BOWANGA (1951/54) 58
THE BOWERY BOYS MEET THE MONSTERS (1954) 16
BRIDE OF THE MONSTER (1955) 20
CAGED (1950) 26, 27
CAPTIVE WOMEN (1952) 75
CAT WOMEN OF THE MOON (1953) 77
CELL 2455 DEATH ROW (1954) 37
UN CHANT D'AMOUR (1950) 108
CONQUEST OF SPACE (1954) 92
CONTINENTE PERDUTO (1955) 121
THE CREATURE FROM THE BLACK LAGOON (1953-54) 3, 78, 79
CULT OF THE COBRA (1955) 21
THE DAY THE EARTH STOOD STILL (1951) 74
THE DAY THE WORLD ENDED (1955) 92
LES DIABOLIQUES (1954) 38
DEMENTIA (1953) 11-12
DESTINATION MOON (1950) 72
DEVIL GIRL FROM MARS (1954) 84, 85
DON QUIXOTE (1955-69) 67
DONOVAN'S BRAIN (1953) 79
DOOMSTOWN USA (1955) 43
DU RIFIFI CHEZ LES HOMMES (1954) 42
EARTH VS THE FLYING SAUCERS (1956) 98
EL ENMASCARADO DE PLATA (1953) 64
ET DIEU... CRÉA LA FEMME (1956) 129
FEITIÇO DO AMAZONAS (1954) 117
THE FEMALE JUNGLE (1954) 39
FIRE MAIDENS FROM OUTER SPACE (1956) 99
FIVE (1951) 74
THE 5,000 FINGERS OF DR. T. (1953) 63
FORBIDDEN PLANET (1956) 100
FOUR SIDED TRIANGLE (1953) 80
THE GARDEN OF EDEN (1954) 117
GIRL GANG (1952) 30
GIRLS IN PRISON (1956) 48

GLEN OR GLENDA (1953) 4, 112
GOJIRA (1954) 86
GORILLA AT LARGE (1954) 17
DIE GÖTTIN VOM RIO BENI (1950) 108
H – THE STORY OF A TEENAGE DRUG ADDICT (1951) 29-30
THE HITCH HIKER (1952) 31
HON DANSADE EN SOMMAR (1951) 110, 111
HOT ROD GIRL (1956) 49
HOUSE OF WAX (1953) 14
INVADERS FROM MARS (1953) 81
INVASION OF THE BODY SNATCHERS (1956) 101
ISSUN-BOSHI (1955) 21
IT CAME FROM BENEATH THE SEA (1955) 94
IT CAME FROM OUTER SPACE (1953) 82
JUJIN YUKI OTOKO (1955) 93
JUNGLE JIM IN PYGMY ISLAND (1950) 56
JUNGLE JIM IN THE FORBIDDEN LAND (1952) 60
JUNGLE MANHUNT (1951) 59
JUNGLE MOON MEN (1955) 67
KAIBYO ARIMA GOTEN (1953) 12, 13
KAIBYO OKAZAKI SODO (1954) 18, 19
KARAMOJA (1954) 118
KILLER APE (1953) 54, 55
KILLERS FROM SPACE (1954) 87
KISS ME DEADLY (1954) 40, 41
LATUKO (1950) 109
LIANE, DAS MÄDCHEN AUS DEM URWALD (1956) 1, 130
LUCRÈCE BORGIA (1953) 113
THE MAD MAGICIAN (1954) 19
MAGIE VERDE (1952) 111
THE MAN FROM PLANET X (1951) 75
THE MAN WITH THE GOLDEN ARM (1955) 44
MARIHUANA: EL TABACO NEGRO DEL DIABLO (1950) 28, 29
MAU MAU (1954) 41
THE MAZE (1953) 15
MESA OF LOST WOMEN (1951-3) 8
THE MOLE PEOPLE (1956) 102, 103
LA MÔME PIGALLE (1955) 121
MONKEY ON THE BACK (1955-56) 45
EL MONSTRUO RESUCITADO (1953) 15
NIGHT OF THE HUNTER (1955) 45-46
NIGHTMARE IN RED CHINA (1954) 41
NOITA PALAA ELÄMÄÄN (1952) 10, 11
NUIT ET BROUILLARD (1955) 46
LOS OLVIDADOS (1950) 29
ONE-WAY TICKET TO HELL (1952/56) 32
ONNA SHINJUO NO FUKUSHU (1956) 131
PANTHER GIRL OF THE KONGO (1955) 68
PREHISTORIC WOMEN (1950) 57
THE PUSHER (c.1955) 46
THE QUATERMASS X-PERIMENT (1955) 95
RADAR MEN FROM THE MOON (1951-52) 76
REBEL WITHOUT A CAUSE (1955) 47
ROCKETSHIP X-M (1950) 73
SADKO (1952) 62
LA SALAIRE DE LA PEUR (1953) 35
SAMBA FANTÁSTICO (1955) 122, 123
SATAN'S WAITIN' (1954) 20
THE SHE-CREATURE (1956) 23
SHICHININ NO SAMURAI (1954) 65

SLASH OF THE KNIFE GOD (1955) 124, 125
SMART ALEC (c.1951) 111
THE SNIPER (1952) 33
SOMMAREN MED MONIKA (1953) 106, 107
SON OF DR. JEKYLL (1951) 6, 7
SPACEWAYS (1953) 83
SWAMP WOMEN (1956) 50
TAIYO NO KISETSU (1956) 51
TARANTULA (1955) 96
TARGET EARTH (1954) 88
TEASERAMA (1955) 126, 127
THE TERRIBLE TRUTH (1951) 30
TEST TUBE BABIES (1953) 113
THEM! (1954) 89
THE THING FROM ANOTHER WORLD (1951) 70, 71
THIS ISLAND EARTH (1955) 96, 97
THREE COMRADES (c.1950) 109
TIJUANA AFTER MIDNITE (1954) 118
TIMESLIP (1955) 96
TOBOR THE GREAT (1954) 90
TÖDLICHE LIEBE (1952-53) 112
LA TOUR DE NESLE (1954-55) 119
TOURBILLON (1953) 114
20,000 LEAGUES UNDER THE SEA (1954) 91
UGETSU MONOGATARI (1953) 65
THE UNDEAD (1956) 24
UNTAMED WOMEN (1952) 61
IL VAMPIRO NEGRO (1953) 35
THE VICE AND THE BADGE (c.1953) 114
VIOLATED (1953) 115
THE VIOLENT YEARS (1956) 52, 53
VOODOO WOMAN (1956) 25
WAR OF THE WORLDS (1953) 84
THE WEREWOLF (1956) 103
THE WILD ONE (1953) 36, 37
WOMEN'S PRISON (1954) 43
THE WONDROUS STORY OF BIRTH (1950) 109
WORLD WITHOUT END (1956) 104
X... THE UNKNOWN (1956) 105
YIELD TO THE NIGHT (1956) 53
ZOMBIES OF THE STRATOSPHERE (1952) 77
ZWERG NASE (1952) 59-60

SHADOWS IN A PHANTOM EYE

ATTRACTIONS & ABERRATIONS IN THE MOVING IMAGE 1872-1949

THE COMPLETE 15-VOLUME SERIES

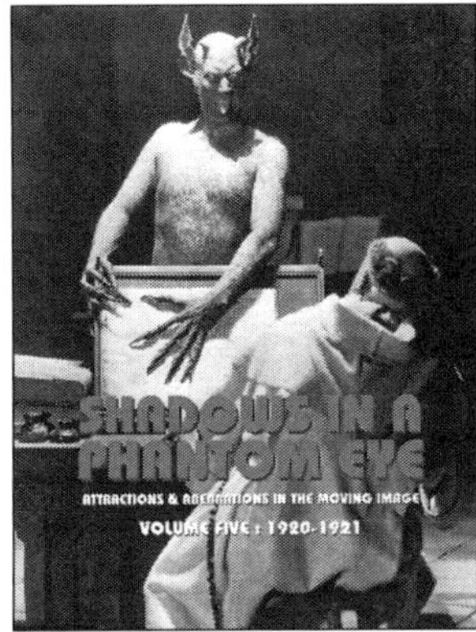

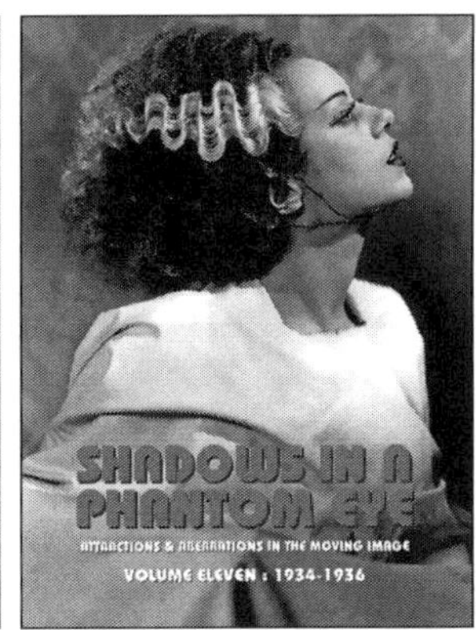